Betty Gillies

WAFS PILOT

The Days and Flights
✝ of a World War II ✝
SQUADRON LEADER

To Daughter
Love
Ma Gillie

Betty Huyler, age 20. She later gave this photo to her good friend and fellow WAFS Barbara "BJ" Erickson. She signed it "To Daughter, Love, Ma Gillies." *Courtesy: Barbara Erickson London's Family Collection*

Betty Gillies
WAFS PILOT

The Days and Flights
✝ of a World War II ✝
SQUADRON LEADER

by Sarah Byrn Rickman

FLIGHT TO DESTINY PRESS
Colorado Springs, CO

ISBN: 978-1-7350595-0-1
Library of Congress Control Number: 2020910465.
Copyright © 2020 Sarah Byrn Rickman. All Rights Reserved.

Published by *Flight to Destiny Press*, Colorado Springs, CO 80907

Cover Image courtesy: *The Gillies Family Collection*
Cover & Interior design by Robert Schram, Bookends Design

Manufactured in the United States of America

Cover caption: Betty Gillies prepares to deliver a P-47 Thunderbolt for the Ferrying Division, Air Transport Command, U.S. Army Air Forces.

Dedication

This book is dedicated to Pete Gillies and Glen Gillies, father and daughter, Betty Huyler Gillies's son and granddaughter. They have shared with me and worked with me in my journey to write Betty's WAFS/WASP World War II story.

Sarah Byrn Rickman, May 17, 2020

Foreword

By Glen J. Gillies

MANY YEARS AGO my grandmother invited me to a WAFS/ WASP reunion luncheon/get-together at a restaurant close to where we lived. I accepted her invitation expecting to walk into a room of intimidating, dynamic, and overwhelming women. What I found was a group of "girls" of all shapes and sizes, some with gray hair, some using canes, all talking and laughing and being happy to be together.

Knowing what I know now I realize I was witnessing the closeness that comes from sharing a special experience with people outside of your "real" life. I met tow target pilots and test pilots, grandmothers, and world travelers. I didn't know what impact that luncheon would have on my life. I was reminded not to judge a book by its cover.

Few of us get the chance to know our parents as people, let alone our grandparents. When my grandmother could no longer travel alone my grandfather enlisted me as her travel companion. Her independent nature resented my intrusion into her world, though she accepted me and introduced me to everyone as her granddaughter, the truck driver. When asked if I was a pilot, she would admit that I was fixed and rotary wing rated. Then she would say that she knew a lot of lady pilots, but not lady truck drivers, and she was proud of me!

I learned so much about her from the women and men I met who admired her and appreciated her contributions through her lifelong support of general aviation, her leadership of the All Woman's Transcontinental Air Race, and her time as a WAFS/ WASP during WWII.

She seemed to not understand what all the fuss was about, why everybody wanted to meet her and speak to her and interview her, because as she would say, "I was just living my life." She wasn't overly humble or modest. She was doing her part for the war effort, for her beloved USA, and she knew she was lucky to have a skill that she enjoyed, and that made a difference.

Grandma was just living her life. Flying a plane was as ordinary to her as driving a car. She did not consider herself extraordinary though she knew that the opportunities that she had were exceptional. She was a patriot and was proud to serve her country in whatever way that she could. She was a skilled pilot, a detail oriented and disciplined person. I can imagine how that discipline strengthened her to do the job that she accepted with the WAFS/WASP.

She cared about her "girls" and she loved to fly. She was direct, no nonsense, and a natural leader. That legacy lives on in the memories of the people I have met over the years that knew her, worked with her, and learned from her. To a person they admired her generosity and strength of character.

When Sarah approached me about wanting to write this book there was only one right answer. Working with my father, Betty's son Pete, has given me the opportunity to spend more time with him and get to know him better, as we both learned about his mother and father and their aviation histories and many contributions.

The woman, the pilot, my Grandma—this is a story of two years of her life of which she was very proud. I feel that the message she would want this book to pass on is to step up, do your job, and do it well, and with dignity and grace step down when the time comes. And, don't underestimate the 'short' people. Stature comes from within, from honing your skills and doing your job with confidence.

So, thanks go out to Sarah Byrn Rickman for initiating this project, for sharing her passion for the history of the WAFS and WASP of World War II and for opening the door to my grandmother's story wider than it has ever been.

Contents

P-38 Lightning *Courtesy: Rancho Runner, GettyImages®*

Chapter One

"On Wings of Gold"

The sun creased the horizon.

Suspended in the bubble-enclosed cockpit of the twin-engine, twin-tailed P-38 Lightning, the pilot pressed her toes hard against the brakes. The aircraft trembled, ready to fly.

Eyes focused on the instrument panel, she watched the dials and gauges that would tell her when the engine reached takeoff power.

"It was still dark and smoggy—a typical morning in Long Beach with dense, low-hanging clouds. I couldn't see very well, but when the control tower said 'go,' I went."

She lifted her toes from the brakes and shoved the throttles to full power, "pouring the coals" to the engines. The surge held her against the seat as the Lightning's wheels rolled faster, faster, faster, gaining momentum. The wind caught beneath the wings and lifted the silver aircraft from the runway. A swirling brownish murk engulfed the plane. The ground vanished.

Now flying blind, she kept her eyes on the instruments in front of her. Her left hand on the throttles, her right hand held the controls that determined the aircraft's upward movement. The silver plane climbed through the darkness.

"At nine hundred feet, the airplane burst through into a cloudless blue sky. The sun's rays hit my silver wings and turned them to gold. I wanted to pull something and stop right there in the air.

1

"Below was fog and black stuff. Directly in front of me were these two snow-covered peaks, well over ten thousand feet, the sun coming up through the pass between them.

"And above it all was this sleek airplane, flying on wings of gold."

The pilot of that United States warplane was 35-year-old Betty Huyler Gillies.

Her destination was the shipping docks at Newark, New Jersey. Flying during daylight only, the trip from Pacific Coast to Atlantic Coast took two days if the weather cooperated. When she landed, Betty taxied the aircraft to her assigned spot, cut the power, and checked that all the dials, gauges, and switches were turned off.

The ground crew took over, removed and stored the wings separately, and prepared the Lightning to be hoisted aboard a waiting Liberty ship, a wartime cargo vessel that would take it to England. From there, the P-38 was destined to fly in the World War II (WWII) battles fought to free Europe from the dominance of Nazi Germany.

Betty climbed down from the cockpit. Carrying her parachute and briefcase, she headed for the Operations Office. There she "sold" the airplane back to the U.S. government. From the time she picked it up in Long Beach until she delivered it and signed it over to the Army, the P-38 belonged to her. For the duration of the flight, the pilot was considered to "own" the plane, and therefore, on landing, "sold" it back.

A Red Cross shuttle bus took her across the Hudson River to New York where she caught a train to Wilmington, Delaware. Betty commanded the squadron of women pilots stationed at New Castle Army Air Base in Wilmington.

At her desk back on base, she awaited her next assignment.

Who was Betty Huyler Gillies? In a time when women seldom worked outside the home, how did a woman happen to be in the cockpit of a U.S. warplane? And why?

Betty Gillies, September 1942. *Courtesy: WASP Archive, Texas Woman's University, Denton*

The "why" was simple given the circumstances. The "how" was more complex.

Early in World War II, the United States did not have enough qualified male pilots to fight the war that had been thrust on it December 7, 1941. That Sunday morning, Japanese warplanes

Nancy Love organized and commanded the Women's Auxiliary Ferrying Squadron.
Courtesy: WASP Archive, Texas Woman's University, Denton

caught the United States, its military, and its people off guard with a bombing attack. Japanese aircraft sank most of the Navy fleet anchored at Pearl Harbor in Honolulu, Hawaii.

Totally unprepared, the United States was plunged into a major war on two fronts. In the Pacific, the country was pitted against the

Empire of Japan. Across the Atlantic, in Europe, America went to war with Japan's ally, Nazi Germany.

The country didn't have enough planes to fight a war, nor did it have enough men to fly those aircraft had they been available. The immediate goal: build more aircraft and train more men to fly them.

Factories geared up and began building trainers in which to teach more men to fly. But because of the current pilot shortage, men could not be found to fly them to the flight schools. So the trainers sat undelivered, therefore idle, at the factories.

Nancy Harkness Love, a well-known and respected 28-year-old woman pilot, met with Colonel William H. Tunner, commander of the Ferrying Division, Air Transport Command, U.S. Army Air Forces. She told him that she knew a number of qualified women flyers capable of ferrying (delivering) those trainers from the factories to the flight schools. Tunner was interested.

He hired her to find qualified women and to organize and lead what became the Women's Auxiliary Ferrying Squadron (WAFS) of World War II.

Twenty-eight women, ages 21 to 35, made up the first squadron. Each woman had at least 500 hours of flying time. Most had more. All had experience in aircraft similar to the primary (beginner) trainers they would ferry from the factories to pilot training sites. The women were civilians, employed through civil service, but they were under military command.

Betty Gillies was the first woman Nancy Love accepted into the squadron. The date was September 10, 1942.

Sixteen months later, Betty Gillies had advanced from flying small single-engine training aircraft to flying one of the United States' most powerful warplanes, the twin-engine P-38 fighter.

How Betty and Nancy and the other WWII women pilots made this happen is the rest of this story.

William H. Tunner (Colonel and later General, U.S. Army Air Forces) *Courtesy: U.S. Air Force*

Chapter Two

"To Catch My Man"

NOTE: DIRECT QUOTES FROM BETTY'S DIARY, *her oral histories, and postwar speeches appear in italics throughout this book.*

"I took up flying for one of the oldest reasons known to womanhood," Betty Gillies said, *"to catch my man."*

Betty's given name was Mildred Elizabeth, and she was born into the Huyler family of Syosset, Long Island, early in 1908.

An event that would alter her life, and the lives of everyone else, had taken place just over four years before. On December 17, 1903, two brothers from Ohio, Orville and Wilbur Wright, successfully flew an "aeroplane"—a winged machine made of wood, fabric, and wire and powered by a gas-operated engine. Mankind had made its first powered flight.

Horses were young Betty's first love. As a child, she worked at becoming an excellent rider. Her adolescent ambition was to ride in New York's Madison Square Garden Horse Show—which she did, several times. But two new loves were waiting just beyond the horizon.

In 1928, twenty-year-old Betty Huyler entered nurses training at Columbia Presbyterian Hospital in New York City. Flying airplanes was not in her plans, until she met Brewster Allison "Bud" Gillies.

Amelia Earhart *Courtesy: The Ninety-Nines Museum of Women Pilots, Oklahoma City*

"I was head-over-heels in love."

Bud was a Navy pilot. Most of their dates were in the company of his Navy buddies. *"All they talked about was flying. I decided that if I wanted to be with him, I had to be able to speak the language."*

Betty shared this predicament with a friend, who handed her a copy of *Cosmopolitan* magazine. "Here, read this," she said. In the magazine was the article "You Too Can Fly," written by the famous American aviatrix (woman pilot) Amelia Earhart.

Betty signed up for half-hour flying lessons at Roosevelt Field on Long Island. The drive between classes at the hospital and the airport was approximately 30 miles via the Long Island motorway and probably took at least 45 minutes. Her first lesson was on November 10, 1928. She flew an OX-5 Travel Air, a popular 1920s flight training aircraft.

Betty Huyler and her Gipsy Moth *Courtesy: Smithsonian National Air and Space Museum* (NASM CW8G-M-0359)

"At that time I was working in the children's ward," Betty said. "I was so enthusiastic about flying, the kids got interested as well. When I got back from a lesson, they asked, 'How do you do it? What kind of control do you have?'

"I'd tell them there was this control stick between your knees. You push it forward if you want to go down. You pull back on it if you want to go up. Every afternoon, I went flying again with the kids in the children's ward."

Seven hours and 35 minutes of flight later, on December 23, Betty soloed the OX-5.

"In those days, we needed only 10 hours of solo for a private license. They didn't have so much to teach us back then. I was able to get my Private License on May 6, 1929. By then I had a total of 22 hours and 55 minutes."

She was hooked.

Nurses training didn't leave much time for flying, so Betty gave up nursing and concentrated on flying—and on Bud Gillies. *"I bought a used Gipsy Moth* so that I could build up my time for my Limited Commercial and then my Transport license. I flew as much as I could that summer."*

Betty's 60-plus-year flying career had begun.

Betty wasn't the only woman to follow Earhart's example and take to the air. By mid-1929, 117 American women had a pilots' license.

In August that year, 20 of them competed in the first official women-only air race in the United States. Betty was not one of them. She did not yet have the required 100 hours of flying time, but she was well aware of the race.

The field of 20 took off from Santa Monica, California, on August 18, destination Cleveland, Ohio. Nine days and 2,700 miles later, well-known aviatrix Louise Thaden won the Heavier Aircraft Division. Veteran flyer Phoebe Omlie won the Lighter Aircraft Division. Humorist of the day Will Rogers christened the race " The Powder Puff Derby." The name stuck.

During the nine-day race, the women began to talk among themselves about forming an Organization of women fliers. After the race, Thaden and Omlie moved the idea forward. They drafted a letter and sent it to all 117 licensed female pilots in the United States, inviting them to join.

On November 2, 1929, Betty, younger than most, joined 25 other licensed female pilots for the group's first meeting, held at Curtiss Field on Long Island. They formed the first pilots' organization for women and sent out a second letter to America's women who flew, asking them to join.

-----

* The de Havilland Gipsy is a British air-cooled four-cylinder in-line aircraft engine. The Gipsy went on to become one of the most popular sport aircraft engines between World War I and World War II. https://en.wikipedia.org/wiki/De_Havilland_Gipsy

The 1929 organizational meeting of The 99s found 26 women gathered in a hangar at Curtiss Airport in Valley Stream, Long Island. Betty Huyler is pictured third from left in the back row. Her head is turned to the right. (Three were absent when the photo was taken, but arrived later.) *Courtesy: The Ninety-Nines Museum of Women Pilots, Oklahoma City*

Ninety-nine responded, and the women took Ninety-Nines as their name in recognition of their charter membership number. Amelia Earhart was elected president and Louise Thaden, secretary. Betty Huyler was one of the charter members.

On November 4, Curtiss Wright Flying Service of New York hired Betty as a saleswoman. Already, she had impressed several of Long Island's male pilots with her flying ability.

"She will sell Gipsy Moths, the same type of plane as that flown by the Prince of Wales," a press release from her new employer stated. "She has adopted flying as a profession. She is an active member of the Long Island Aviation Country Club and recently won a spot landing contest* in competition with twenty men."

---

*Spot landing contest: a white line is placed 50 feet from the approach end of the runway. Each contestant makes two landings, as close to the designated landing spot as possible. The individual with the two landings closest to the line wins

"October 21, 1929, Betty Huyler wins the spot landing contest besting 20 men." The occasion was the first society air meet held at Long Island's Aviation Country Club. *Courtesy: Cradle of Aviation Museum, Garden City, New York*

Betty had 130 hours of flight time in her logbook.

Curtiss Wright hired four other charter Ninety-Nines as well. On November 19, Betty, Fay Gillis, Frances Harrell, Ruth Nichols, and Neva Paris took part in a fashion show modeling "flying clothing" at

An aviation fashion show "Flying Colors" featured Betty Huyler and fellow Ninety-Nines charter members Frances Harrell, Fay Gillis, and Neva Paris. Photo on the right: Betty Huyler dressed for a 1929 social occasion. *Courtesy: The Gillies Family Collection, news clipping from the November 19, 1929, issue of the New York American*

The Plaza Hotel in New York City. The show made the newspaper's society pages.

A new job wasn't all that was happening in Betty's life.

"*Then, of course, I married the guy,*" Betty said, "*which was well worth the effort.*"

Chapter Three

The WAFS Gather

September 1942

AIR TRANSPORT COMMAND (ATC) commanding officer General Harold L. George received the go-ahead he had been waiting for. Nancy Love could begin recruiting. Telegrams went out to 83 women Nancy thought could qualify to fly Army training aircraft from factories to flight training schools.

Betty's telegram arrived at the Gillies household in Syosset, New York, on September 6. *"What should I do?"* Betty asked Bud.

"Isn't this just what you've been preparing for and wanting to do?" Bud asked. *"Go, of course."*

Betty held a twin-engine rating and an instrument rating (meaning she could fly without visual reference to the ground) and had 1,261 hours in her logbook. The following morning, she embarked on what became the greatest adventure of her life.

Betty and her friend, Barbara Kibbee (Kib) Jayne, took off in Betty and Bud's single-engine Fairchild for DuPont Field in Wilmington, Delaware. Their destination was New Castle Army Air Base (NCAAB) to learn just what might be expected of them if they joined this new group.

Wartime flight regulations were in effect along the entire coast-line of the United States. Pilots had to file a flight plan with a valid

Nancy Love sends Betty Gillies off for her test flight in a PT-19 primary trainer.
Courtesy: The Love Family Collection

reason for all flights, so Betty and Kib declared theirs to be an instrument training flight.

On the trip down, Betty flew "under the hood"* in order to practice her instrument flying skills. Kib acted as Betty's safety pilot. On the trip back, Kib flew under the hood with Betty as lookout.

They reported to NCAAB Headquarters and found Nancy Love. *"We talked for about an hour, then headed home. I told Nancy I would be down again Thursday for a flight test."*

On September 10, Betty returned. Kib, who had a flying job with Grumman Aircraft, decided not to join.

"Went down to Wilmington on the train. Weather lousy all a.m. but cleared in time for me to get my check flight with Lt. Joe Tracy in a Fairchild trainer. We were out about 50 minutes."

Nancy and Betty had a long talk. Betty was convinced. She wrote in her diary: *"So, I guess I am going to join the WAFS!* [Women's Auxiliary Ferrying Squadron] *Bud thinks it's very worthwhile trying out, and so do I. We have to sign up for 3-month stretches and duty begins on the 21st."*

The next day, a call from Nancy Love sent Betty back to Wilmington immediately. *"She requested my presence at 8 o'clock tomorrow morning for pictures!"*

Betty boarded the 10 p.m. train that night and arrived in Wilmington long after midnight. She spent what was left of the night at Wilmington's DuPont Hotel and was out at the airbase by eight the next morning. She found two photographers from two national news organizations—*Pathé News* and *Life* magazine— already there!

---

*A black cloth hood restricts outside visibility for the pilot. The copilot acts as the safety pilot, or lookout. This is how instrument flight training was taught then.

Ready to sign up: The first four women pilots to join Nancy Love's original WAFS: Cornelia Fort, Helen Mary Clark, Aline "Pat" Rhonie and Betty Gillies *Courtesy Robert Patterson, grandson of Col. Robert H. Baker, 2nd Ferrying Group Commander*

"So far there are five of us. We got sworn in and had lunch at the Officers Mess with Nancy. Am scheduled to go 'on duty' on the 21st— I'm 'on leave' 'til then!"

Betty took the next week to make arrangements for her family. She didn't know how long she would be gone, but a minimum 90-day sign-up was required. Bud's mother would stay with the children and help out. On September 20, Bud drove Betty to New York City's Penn Station. She took the train to Wilmington.

September 21: *"Out at NCAAB bright and early."*

Four WAFS in military issue coveralls: Helen Mary Clark, Aline "Pat" Rhonie,
Catherine Slocum, and Cornelia Fort *Courtesy: Robert Patterson, grandson of Colonel
Robert H. Baker, 2nd Ferrying Group commander*

Nine women now made up the WAFS unit. Betty and Nancy
had been joined by Cornelia Fort, Aline Rhonie, Helen Mary
Clark, Catherine Slocum, Esther Nelson, Del Scharr, and Teresa
James. They were issued khaki flight coveralls that were made to fit
men—and far too large for most of the women—a parachute, gog-
gles, a white silk Army Air Forces flying scarf, and a leather flying
jacket.

"We spent today getting our equipment, being fitted for our 'chutes'
[parachutes] *fixing our rooms, etc. All we had to wear were those coveralls.*

"We are living in what used to be a BOQ [Bachelor Officers Quarters]—a long green barn, which looked awfully bare and cold this morning but looks much better tonight, after we fixed it up a bit."

BOQ 14 was a two-story wooden barracks with 44 square-shaped rooms, each equipped with an iron cot, Army blankets, a bureau, a large pine wardrobe with no door, and blue scatter rugs. In addition, BOQ 14 sported the only Venetian blinds on the base, providing privacy for the women whose only other option was to undress in the dark.

Partitions also were added to the formerly open shower stalls and commodes in the bathroom. Washbasins lined one wall, each topped by a pine shelf, with mirrors. Workmen had knocked out walls on each floor to provide a lounge for the women.

"BOQ 14 was rather drafty. My room was on the northeast corner. I could see daylight through several of the cracks—but I loved it! We were right in the center of the base and next to the Officers Club, which we were privileged to enjoy."

Betty was in awe of the base. *"This huge airport with all the fantastic flying machines scattered about."*

The next morning, *"Up at 6:45 on duty at 8. Devoted the entire day to newsreels, photographers and reporters! By order of the War Department! Got fitted for standardized attire [clothing]. Tomorrow we start work—I hope!"*

Base commander Colonel Robert H. Baker welcomed them. Their designation on base was Civilian Pilots.

"I like Colonel Baker very much and believe he likes having us under his command. He certainly did everything he could to provide comfortable and convenient quarters for us. He saw to it that we ate our meals in the Officers' Mess and were welcome at the Officers Club. I felt that the WAFS were accepted without question."

Baker announced that the WAFS would stand in formation for roll call with the men at 8 a.m. each morning. Then he added that

2nd Ferrying Group Commander, Colonel Robert H. Baker *Courtesy: Robert Patterson, grandson of Colonel Robert H. Baker, 2nd Ferrying Group commander*

he expected the women to march in Saturday morning review along with the men of the base.

Marching in formation was not what most of them expected when they signed up to fly. The order didn't faze Betty.

"I was a drill sergeant at Ogontz, the prep school I attended," she told the others at an after-hours bull session in the BOQ. *"We marched on the hockey field and carried heavy guns made of wood."*

Nancy Love and Colonel Baker review the WAFS: from left, Betty Gillies, Esther Nelson, Cornelia Fort, Teresa James, Catherine Slocum, Del Scharr, Helen Mary Clark, and Aline Rhonie. *Courtesy: International Women's Air and Space Museum, Cleveland, Ohio*

This elicited blank stares from all but one other. Cornelia Fort had attended the same school. She chimed in, "Ogontz was the only girls' school I know of with military battalions—three of them."

Betty was 10 years Cornelia's senior, but both were graduates of the fashionable Philadelphia finishing school, which was also Amelia Earhart's prep school alma mater.

"I should have been kicked out of that school for things I did," Betty admitted to the other WAFS as the conversation continued. *"The seniors at Ogontz got to have parties in the woods and we undergrads would slip out and heckle them. We climbed down the slate roof to where the garbage truck came in and slid down from there.*

"One night we got caught. The headmistress threatened to stay in my room all night to keep me there, 'unless you promise you won't go out again.'

"I promised."

Nancy Love was the squadron's disciplinarian. At first, she also had to oversee BOQ 14 as a women's residence. But she and Colonel Baker soon hired Mrs. Anderson to serve as housemother and manager. "Andy," as the WAFS called her, became a fixture and a friend to the women of BOQ 14.

On September 23 the WAFS 30-day orientation began.

The women received 25 hours of flight instruction plus 72 hours of ground school made up of a review of communications, navigation, meteorology, power plants [engines], military forms, military law, and military drill.

"*Each of us got to fly an L-2B* [small training aircraft] *for 50 minutes. Did some Figure Eights* [using the airplane's exhaust to draw figure eights in the sky], *made three landings, then some forced landings. Came down completely discouraged!*

"*Our instructors don't seem to agree as to where and how we fly, which confounds us no end! The next day was more of the same. Wind about 25 mph, weather clear, beautiful.*

"*Today the wind blew a gale all day. I made one uncomfortable solo flight over to DuPont Field and practiced landings. Was out about 55 minutes. Taxiing in a crosswind* [wind blowing directly across the runway or at an angle to it] *was too ticklish to be fun—I feared for the wing tips!*"

By September 30 life in the WAFS was off to a good start. Betty and Nancy began to spend more time together. That's when Betty learned how her friend happened to be in the right place at the right time and had ended up at NCAAB in command of a small contingent of civilian women pilots.

Chapter Four

Why Were the WAFS Needed?

AFTER THE ATTACK ON PEARL HARBOR, airfields within 50 miles of the U.S. coastline were shut down. That included East Boston Airport where Nancy and her husband, Robert M. Love, owned and ran Inter City Aviation. They sold airplanes, gave flight instruction, and did charter flights. Nancy frequently ferried an aircraft to a buyer in another city. But now, because of the shutdown, they were out of business.

Bob Love was in the Air Corps Reserve. He was ordered to active duty with the Air Transport Command in Washington, D.C. Nancy followed him to Washington. Not wanting to sit on the sidelines of the war, she went to work.

March 11, 1942, then Major Robert H. Baker, in command of the district ferrying operation in Baltimore, Maryland, hired her as a civilian employee. She had worked hand in hand with Bob at Inter City Aviation for more than five years and knew aviation inside and out. Baker made her his Operations Manager.

Now, Nancy was witness to the growing production of military aircraft. At the same time, she recognized that there were not nearly enough male pilots to move all those planes coming off the assembly lines, many of which were small training aircraft. She suggested to Baker that they recruit highly qualified women pilots to ferry those trainers.

Baker referred her to his boss, General George, head of the Air Transport Command. George supported Nancy's suggestion. Then on May 29, Baker's command, including Nancy, was moved to newly constructed New Castle Army Air Base. He was promoted to colonel and placed in command of the base.

Baker answered to Colonel Tunner, who led the Ferrying Division, the major arm of General George's Air Transport Command. This is when Tunner, the man responsible for finding those badly needed ferry pilots, met Nancy Love and the idea of the WAFS was born.

On June 11, 1942, General George sent a memo to Army Air Forces Headquarters stating that it was time to use qualified women to ferry airplanes for the Ferrying Division, "in so far as qualified women are available."

Many years later in a speech to a younger generation of women involved in aviation, Betty Gillies summed up Tunner and the Ferrying Division's decision: *"They wanted to determine the suitability of using women pilots in the delivery of military aircraft."*

It took three more months for the WAFS to become a reality. When Betty received her telegram September 6, inviting her to join the squadron at New Castle Army Air Base, the program was a go.

✢ ✢ ✢

The WAFS made their first ferrying flight October 23-24, 1942. Nancy appointed Betty flight leader. Cornelia Fort, Helen Mary Clark, Aline Rhonie, Del Scharr, Teresa James, and Betty boarded a twin-engine transport aircraft, piloted by Colonel Baker, for the short flight to the Piper Aircraft factory in Lock Haven, Pennsylvania.

Their assignment: take six L-4B Cubs* from Lock Haven to Mitchel Field on Long Island.

L-4B Piper Cub *Courtesy: iStock by Getty Images*

Women were a big part of the workforce at Piper Aircraft. The sight of these six women, wearing their WAFS uniforms, sent a positive message to the Piper gals. They watched as the WAFS inspected their ships, climbed into the cockpits, and took off. Eventually, several Piper women would learn to fly the Army way with the Women's Flying Training Detachment school currently being formed in Texas.

"That night we RONed (remained overnight) in a hotel in Allentown, Pennsylvania," Teresa James recalled. "We had been thoroughly trained and familiarized with how to fill out the necessary RON forms."

The next morning, Betty, familiar with the look of the greater New York area from the air, led the flight into Mitchel Field. When she signed the planes over, an ill-tempered officer-of-the-day informed her that he needed them two months ago, not now.

"That's not my problem," Teresa recalled Betty saying. "I'm merely following orders. You may speak to my commanding officer,

---

*The L-4B was a 65-horsepower, single-engine, two-seat airplane. The "L" stood for liaison, a connection or means of communication. These small aircraft served as a "connecting" link for communication between commands.

Nancy Love wearing the WAFS dress uniform
that she designed *Courtesy: The Love Family Collection*

Colonel Robert Baker at New Castle Army Air Base, or call
Colonel Tunner himself at Ferrying Division headquarters."

By the time the women began to report for duty in Wilmington,
Nancy Love had decided on the WAFS official uniform. It consist-
ed of a tailored gray wool jacket with squared shoulders, brass but-
tons, a detached belt, and matching skirt and slacks. The six
women who made that first ferrying flight were the first to wear the
new uniform with slacks in public.

In 1942 the world was not used to seeing women in slacks. They
were refused entrance to most dining establishments and many
other places as well. The only answer was for women attired in
trousers to accept the snub and hope for a more liberal policy else-

The WAFS study up on their aeronautical charts in preparation for a trip: on the floor (from left), Gertrude Meserve and Betty Gillies; seated (from left), Nancy Batson, Teresa James, Esther Nelson, and Dorothy Fulton. *Courtesy: WASP Archive, Texas Woman's University, Denton*

where. The WAFS were not out to prove they could wear pants. They only wanted to prove they could fly.

✦ ✦ ✦

In November the WAFS squadron stood at 20. New arrivals were Barbara Poole, Helen Richards, Barbara Towne, Gertrude Meserve, Florene Miller, Barbara Jane "BJ" Erickson, Delphine Bohn, Barbara Donahue, Evelyn Sharp, Phyllis Burchfield, Esther Manning, and Nancy Batson. Catherine Slocum had left after graduation in October. She had children at home, and the woman she and her husband had hired to take care of them was ill.

Now the squadron ferrying began in earnest. Nancy sent out eight to 10 women at a time. Since they were ferrying slower airplanes that needed to refuel frequently, it was easier to fly in groups.

"We're waiting for eight Cubs," Betty wrote in her diary November 2. "They're supposed to be ready for delivery, but no orders have come as to where to take them. So we sit."

On November 9 the Cubs were ready. The WAFS headed for Lock Haven, this time to ferry planes south.

Disaster struck when they landed in Charlottesville, Virginia. The field was a sea of mud. Cornelia Fort's and Barbara Poole's planes nosed over, resulting in two bent propellers.

When tall, lanky Helen Richards stepped out of her Cub, she sank knee-deep into the mire. Neither she nor her plane were the worse for wear, but her new uniform slacks were covered with mud and her shoes were ruined. The Army had not supplied the women with boots, so they wore whatever footwear they had.

"The rest of us got down by the grace of the good gremlins," Betty wrote, then added, "The Men's Room became a Ladies Room—proudly donated without our request!"

Leaving Fort and Poole and their damaged aircraft behind, the other WAFS headed for their various destinations. Saturday night, Betty, BJ Erickson, and Teresa James RONed in New Orleans.

In the fall of 1942, Betty Gillies and BJ were in the process of establishing what would become a lifelong friendship. Betty, 12 years older than BJ, recognized the leadership potential in this outstanding young woman. BJ, in later years, delighted in telling the story of how Betty introduced her to some of the finer things in life.

> That night in New Orleans, Betty treated me to dinner at the famous restaurant, Antoine's. This was a gorgeous restaurant. Dim lights, mood music in the background, the waiters immaculate in tuxes and ties.

Helen Richards *Courtesy: Dorothy Scott Family Collection*

She ordered the house specialty, Oysters Rockefeller, for both of us. My first time there. I'd never heard of, let alone eaten, Oysters Rockefeller. Well, our waiter put the Oysters Rockefeller in front of us.

I don't particularly care for spinach, particularly when it's messed up. So, very carefully, I took my fork and pushed the spinach off the top and ate the oysters. The waiter was aghast. He was horrified that I was pulling all the Rockefeller off the oysters.

I humiliated poor ol 'Ma.'

She said, 'Daughter, just eat it!' We were calling each other 'mother' and 'daughter' by that time.

Prior to November 22, the WAFS had only ferried Cubs. That day, they received their first assignment to deliver the primary trainers they had been hired to ferry. Once again, Nancy assigned Betty flight leader. They were to pick up the aircraft at Fairchild Aviation in Hagerstown, Maryland.

"*Orders came through this afternoon and caught me completely unprepared. I had half an hour to get ready. Eight of us—Del Scharr, Esther Nelson, Helen Mary Clark, Evelyn Sharp, Florene Miller, Erickson, James and I—took the train to Baltimore.*

"*No bus to Hagerstown until morning. I got in touch with Group Operations to tell them.*"

The WAFS slept in the bus station, propped against their parachutes.

"*We caught the 7 a.m. bus to Hagerstown. There, visibility was zero. Off to the hotel where we spent the day. That night, Del Scharr came down with a bad throat, chills and fever. Called a doctor in to see her.*"

The next day Betty wrote: "*Still in Hagerstown. Three more WAFS arrived this a.m. Richards, Burchfield and Batson. We took Scharr to the local hospital. We expect to get out tomorrow. Didn't want to leave her alone in the hotel.*"

Six WAFS in fleece-lined flight suits, at Hagerstown, Maryland, to pick up open-cockpit PT-19s: from left are Betty Gillies, Nancy Batson, Esther Nelson, Helen Mary Clark, Teresa James, and Evelyn Sharp, and Captain Franks, Operations Officer. *Courtesy: WASP Archive, Texas Woman's University, Denton*

On November 25 Betty wrote in her diary: *"Finally off this morning at 9:15. Landed Spartanburg at 11:55. The weatherman reported a cold front ahead. We won't be able to get through. Today is Thanksgiving. We went into town and fooled away the afternoon, ate our holiday dinner, went bowling, and got to bed early.*

"Off today at 8:45. The cold front has passed and is it cold! The flight to Chattanooga in open cockpit planes was agony! Delivered Union City, Tennessee, that afternoon. Mission Completed!"

A bus took them to Memphis where an airline limousine picked them up and took them to the airport. *"But, our plane that was to take us back to Philadelphia was late. How we wished for bed! Finally in the air at 3:45 a.m."*

They were back at NCAAB November 28, only to learn they were going out again the following day. Ten WAFS, including Betty, were back to ferrying Cubs. Again, Colonel Baker flew them to Lock Haven.

"Left Lock Haven this morning. Richards, Sharp, Erickson and I RONed in Richmond. Red Cross Motor Corps gave us transportation into town."

And so ended November, the WAFS first full month of ferrying duty.

Ice storms, ceilings with zero visibility, and generally bad weather across the eastern half of the United States refused to go away. Betty and some of the others did not deliver their Cubs for several days. They didn't make it back to base until December 10. Thirteen days! Betty did admit that she finished most of her Christmas shopping while grounded in several places.

"Back in BOQ 14. Mission Finally Completed!" she wrote.

The WAFS were learning about the unpredictable life of a ferry pilot.

Chapter Five

Cochran: "We Need More Women Pilots"

IN APRIL 1942 well-known pilot Jacqueline Cochran—at the suggestion of United States Army Air Forces (USAAF) Commanding General Henry H. "Hap" Arnold—had taken 25 of America's best women pilots to England to fly for the Air Transport Auxiliary. The ATA, as it was called, was a small group of British women ferrying aircraft for the British Royal Air Force (RAF). Women from Canada and other countries were volunteering to fly with them.

The American women took a ship across the dangerous waters of the Atlantic Ocean—dangerous because German submarines patrolled the route, sinking ships headed for England.

Cochran, who wanted to lead all American women pilots selected to serve in WWII, came back to the States in September 1942. The announcement of the WAFS' formation had just been made public. Not pleased with the news, Cochran headed for General Arnold's office and convinced him that one squadron of WAFS wasn't nearly the number of women pilots who could be of use to the USAAF in wartime. She persuaded him to approve the training of more women at an Army flight facility and to put her in charge of it.

The Women's Flying Training Detachment (WFTD) was established mid-November at the Houston, Texas, Municipal Airport.

Jacqueline Cochran in her WASP uniform *Courtesy: Coachella Valley Historical Museum, Indio, California*

Cochran recruited her first class from the remaining women in the United States known to have 200 or more flight hours. There weren't very many, so she accepted women who had fewer than 200 hours but whom she thought could qualify. When they graduated from training the women were to be sent to ferry aircraft with Nancy Love's WAFS.

Five more women had joined the WAFS by the end of November 1942, bringing Nancy's squadron to 25: Katherine Rawls Thompson, Dorothy Fulton, Opal "Betsy" Ferguson, Bernice Batten, and Dorothy Scott.

USAAF Commanding General Henry H. "Hap" Arnold
Courtesy: U.S. Air Force

On December 6 Nancy Love left NCAAB in the company of several ATC officers. They were on their way to visit the other six ATC ferrying bases to see which ones might be suitable—and willing—to house a squadron of women ferry pilots. Betty, as Nancy's second in command, was in charge while she was gone.

From December 14 to 17, the WAFS were off on another Cub delivery. Betty wrote, *"Five WAFS departed for Lock Haven this evening. The train was late, so we sat in the Wilmington Station for 2½ hours. Finally took the 11:30 to Philadelphia, there catching the 1:08 a.m. for Lock Haven."*

But the next day it snowed all day. The five—Cornelia Fort, Dorothy Fulton, Helen Richards, Evelyn Sharp, and Betty—sat around all day. Then on December 16, the five took off, each headed in a different direction.

"I took off headed for Syracuse, NY, but stopped for gas at Ithaca en route. Five minutes after I got on the ground it started to blizzard. Temp zero degrees! I gave up and RONed there. Snow squalls the next morning held me up, so I didn't get off until 11:40. Ran into more squalls, but delivered my Cub to Syracuse this afternoon.

"Then I spent three hours trying to get the airplane signed for! More darned 'passing the buck.' Finally got squared away and was driven into town by a staffer. Caught the 4:50 train, RON NYC."

Betty caught the early morning train out of New York and was back on the job in her office at NCAAB by noon. The next day she sent five of the WAFS to Hagerstown to pick up PT-19s and take them to Texas.

"They were tickled pink!"

On December 21 Dorothy Scott and Bernice Batten, the last two WAFS still in Army orientation, were released for ferrying.

When Nancy Love returned to Wilmington from her two-week inspection tour, Betty met her for dinner in town. "Boy, did she have a lot of news. There are to be three more WAFS bases—Detroit, Dallas, and Long Beach. Five girls from here are going to be sent each place."

Betty made it home for Christmas with her family. The visit was short. On December 28 she was back on base. "Poured rain all day! Six of us got orders to take L-4Bs to Greenville, South Carolina, but departure postponed. Helen Schmidt McGilvery came in to apply for membership. She looks like a good one."

On December 29 Betty noted in her diary that the rain still poured and the BOQ was "an ocean of mud."

The Cub trip was canceled the following day. "Word came that all L-4Bs will now be shipped instead of flown! A PT trip is now pending.

And Colonel Baker told me that within 30 days I will be flying the P-47!* *He was quite serious. I'm going to get Bud to make me some rudder extensions."*

At 5 feet 1½ inches, Betty could not reach the rudder pedals of the P-47. She would need something to help her reach and control the rudders with her feet. A friend of Bud's at Grumman Aircraft— a man not much taller than Betty—had built rudder extension blocks for himself in order to fly bigger aircraft. At Bud's request, the man made a set of the blocks for Betty.

The year ended on a good note. On New Year's Eve Betty wrote, *"Nancy left today to be stationed in Dallas. The other four— Richards, Scott, Miller and Ferguson—leave tomorrow."* Nancy Love had appointed Florene Miller squadron leader in Dallas as Nancy herself, planned to travel between her four squadrons as needed.

"Helen Mary Clark and I played hooky and left on the 4:42 train. She went home to see her family in New Jersey, and I met Bud in NYC to spend New Year's Eve together."

---

* The Republic Aircraft P-47 Thunderbolt, when fully loaded, weighed eight tons. The biggest of the pursuits, it was effective as a short- to medium-range escort fighter in high-altitude air-to-air combat and ground attack in both the European and Pacific theaters.

Betty and her second-in-command, Helen Mary Clark, in the office at NCAAB
Courtesy: WASP Archive, Texas Woman's University, Denton

Chapter Six

P-47 Checkout

BEFORE NANCY LEFT, she named Betty to lead the NCAAB WAFS squadron. Betty wrote in her diary, "*My title now is Commanding WAFS 2nd Ferrying Group!*" Betty promptly appointed Helen Mary Clark her second-in-command. She also named capable and efficient Esther Manning to be her office assistant.

One event marred the New Year. Aline Rhonie had taken an extra day's leave without permission from Colonel Baker. He dismissed her. She countered and resigned.

January 2: "*Review this morning. Goodness knows why, but suddenly the morale of the WAFS at NCAAB is sky high! It does look like we are going to fly bigger and better airplanes!*

"*There are 14 of us back on base and it's like old home week! The biggest group we've had together since we ended our training and started ferrying!*"

That afternoon, Betty talked with Captain Onas Matz. He confirmed that Colonel Baker was ready for her to begin P-47 transition. As soon as Betty had her rudder extensions, she could begin her journey to check out (be approved to fly) the P-47 Thunderbolt.

To qualify, Betty began to fly a series of increasingly bigger, heavier, more complex aircraft as she worked her way up the transition ladder.

WAFS Esther Manning was Betty's Operations Officer.
Courtesy: WASP Archive, Texas Woman's University, Denton

January 3: *"Had another applicant come in today, Kathryn "Sis" Bernheim."* Within days, the review board approved Helen McGilvery and Sis Bernheim.

On January 12 the WAFS who were to form the new squadron at Romulus, Michigan, were busy packing. Barbara Poole, Katherine Thompson, Del Scharr, Barbara Donahue, and Phyllis Burchfield were assigned to the 3rd Ferrying Group at Wayne County Airport outside Detroit. Nancy Love appointed Scharr to lead the group.

A few days later, Nancy Love flew to Romulus to help Scharr get set up. While there, Nancy checked out 35-year-old Lenore

McElroy, wife of a Romulus ferry pilot. Lenore had 3,500 hours as a flight instructor and easily qualified. Just in time, as it turned out.

A surprise announcement came January 25. AAF Headquarters issued a new ruling. As of that day, the Ferrying Division/Air Transport Command would only be allowed to hire women pilots who were graduates of the Women's Flying Training Detachment directed by Jacqueline Cochran. McElroy was WAFS #28, the last woman admitted to Nancy Love's original squadron.

Betty wrote in her diary, *"Looks like Jackie is getting the WAFS under her thumb after all!"*

On February 11 the WAFS threw a going-away party for their squadron mates headed for the 6th Ferrying Group, Long Beach, California. On Betty's wholehearted recommendation, Nancy Love named BJ Erickson squadron commander. Cornelia Fort, Barbara Towne, Evelyn Sharp, and Bernice Batten were going with her.

Betty wrote, *"Sure will miss them."* Betty also noted that Nancy Love was relocating from Dallas to Long Beach. There, Nancy planned to check out in aircraft she hoped the WAFS eventually would fly. Most were built by manufacturers in the Los Angeles Basin.

Bad weather descended on NCAAB and closed the field for several days. Betty's P-47 transition slowed to a crawl. She busied herself in the office. Finally...

> *The weather improved. I'm all steamed up again. I went over to Base Operations and asked if they had an AT-6 [advanced trainer] that needed exercise. Much to my surprise, they gave me one. The captain asked me to fly Lieutenant Schwab over to Middletown so that he could pick up an AT-12.*
>
> *Because Schwab is one of the top pursuit pilots, it would be considered a "check flight" for the P-47. Had a good trip over and all went well. Thank goodness!*

Betty welcomed Helen McGilvery and Kathryn "Sis" Bernheim to the WAFS in early January 1943. *McGilvery photo courtesy: Robert Patterson, grandson of Colonel Robert H. Baker.*

Big news February 27! Nancy Love had flown the P-51.* She was the first woman in the United States to fly a pursuit (fighter) aircraft. Betty took note. With her progress in the P-47, she knew she would be the next.

On March 1, Betty wrote:

> "I 'checked out' in the AT-9 this a.m. and put in an hour solo! Also got a cockpit check in the P-47 by Lieutenant

---

*The P-51 North American Aviation Mustang is a long range, single-engine, single-seat fighter.

"Sis" Bernheim, *Bernheim photo courtesy: WASP Archive,*
Texas Woman's University, Denton

Schwab! Now all I have to do is get in some more landings in
the AT-6 and I'll be qualified to check out in the 47!

"Spent today in the hangar putting the final touches on my
P-47 rudder extensions. Then, at five o'clock, I got an AT-6
and shot landings [made several landings in a row]. *All went*
well. So, I guess I'm qualified to check out in the 47."

On March 4 Captain McKay sent Betty to the Republic
Aviation factory in Farmingdale, Long Island, for the day. There,
an officer introduced her to the P-47 Thunderbolt.

"In the hangar, I sat in the cockpit and he raised the airplane off the
ground so that I could play with the landing gear equipment. He answered
every question I could think of so that, when I got in that airplane to fly it,

The P-51 Mustang. *Courtesy: National Museum of the U.S. Air Force*

*I knew I could reach and handle the equipment. I'm so short, I definitely
needed my rudder pedals."*

Back at NCAAB, Captain McKay wanted to see her rudder extensions and how she fit in the cockpit of the P-47. *"I started one of the ships
and taxied it around on the apron and then out on the runway. Managed OK.
He said I can fly one tomorrow. Now, if only the weather will hold out good!"*

On March 8, 1943, Betty Gillies became the first woman to fly
the P-47.

*"Today was clear but very windy and gusty. I flew the P-47 for one
hour! Took off at 11:20, played around upstairs for 30 minutes and then
shot two landings. Got it back all in one piece! Sure did get a kick out of
it and it sure did keep me busy!"*

The evening of March 11, Betty and Esther Manning (now
Rathfelder) had dinner together in Wilmington. *"We had oysters at
McCaffey's and green salad at the DuPont Hotel. Good!*

The P-47 Thunderbolt *Courtesy: National Museum of the U.S. Air Force*

"Then Esther broke the news to me that she was pregnant!"

Being pregnant meant Esther would be grounded (not allowed to fly). But did it also mean Betty would lose her very able assistant on whom she depended? The following day, Betty told Colonel Baker about Esther. Then she asked him a very big question and got the answer she hoped for.

"He is going to let her stay, but on ground status!"

This meant Esther—who, as a WAFS, was a civilian and lived off base with her AAF husband—could remain as an employee. *"She starts tomorrow as my Assistant Operations Officer. She will hold down my office from 8 to 5. I am free to ferry again!"*

Baker gave Betty more good news. *"He actually wants me to ferry P-47s. But first I will have to log 35 hours in the ship. So, I need to 'put in my time' and fly."*

Betty tries out the cockpit of a P-47. *Courtesy: International Women's Air and Space Museum, Cleveland, Ohio*

Chapter Seven

A 3 a.m. Phone Call

A TELEPHONE CALL in the middle of the night is never good news.

On March 22, at 3 a.m., Betty received a call from Nancy Love. Cornelia Fort, the third woman to join the WAFS, had died in a mid-air collision in Texas.

She was ferrying a BT-13 (basic trainer aircraft) from California to Dallas when a male pilot, also ferrying a BT-13 and thought to be doing aerobatics (stunt maneuvers in the air), clipped the wing of Cornelia's aircraft with the wheel of his landing gear. Part of the wing snapped off and her aircraft immediately went into a fatal dive. Cornelia died on impact. Her plane did not burn. The male pilot landed safely.

Cornelia had survived the December 7, 1941, attack on Pearl Harbor. She was a flight instructor in Honolulu, flying with a student, when the Japanese Zeros appeared out of nowhere. She had landed the plane safely, but not before collecting a few bullet holes in her yellow trainer.

Now Cornelia had become the first woman pilot to die in the line of duty for the U.S. military.* The inscription on her footstone in Nashville's Mount Olivet Cemetery reads: "Killed in the Service of Her Country."

---

*The women pilots of World War II were granted retroactive military status in 1977 (https://airandspace.si.edu/explore). See Author's Note on Pages 177-178 for more on Cornelia Fort.

Cornelia Fort *Courtesy: WASP Archive, Texas Woman's University, Denton*

Cornelia was cleared of any blame in the fatal accident.

Each of the WAFS grieved in her own way, but the women ferry pilots did not let Cornelia's death stop them from continuing to do what they were hired to do—ferry aircraft.

✝ ✝ ✝

On March 30 Betty completed her required 35 hours in the P-47. *"Now all I have left to do is the cross-country,"* she wrote in her diary. *"And Helen Mary Clark starts P-47 transition tomorrow!"*

Betty anticipated more good news.

"I'm excited about a possible flight to Alberta, Canada, in PT-26s [PT-19s with enclosed cockpits]. *But the ships aren't ready yet and we have no guarantee that we'll get the trip."*

On April 7 Betty was assigned to her first P-47 cross-country trip. *"Lt. Schwab, flying a P-39* [also a pursuit], *led the flight of our three P-47s making the trip. I am now 'qualified' to ferry P-47s!"*

As a result, Betty was issued a new piece of equipment. *"This morning, I acquired a .45 automatic pistol from Ordnance. I am to tote it when I ferry '47s. Right now, I am toting it around the BOQ to get used to it—so I can wear it in public with a straight face. More darned fun!"*

Many of the pursuit aircraft carried secret equipment on board, like advanced bombsights, radios, and, later, radar equipment. All the male pursuit-qualified ferry pilots were issued a .45-mm handgun for security. Now women ferry pilots who qualified for pursuit aircraft would be issued a .45-mm automatic and trained to use it.

"In case of capture, shoot the airplane," said WAFS Nancy Batson, who enjoyed sport shooting. "Those were our instructions. The powers-that-be didn't want any of those secret installations captured, so they told us, 'Aim for this little red button'." The little red button was installed to be used by a combat pilot to destroy the aircraft in case of impending capture.

April 16, the Alberta flight was on, and it was Betty's!

This afternoon we got orders! Deliver PT-26s to DeWinton Airport, Calgary, Alberta, Canada!!! Scheduled to leave at 8 a.m. tomorrow, weather permitting. My flight consists of Nancy Batson, Sis Bernheim and Helen McGilvery. [Teresa James led a second flight with Dorothy Fulton and Gertrude Meserve.]

Palm Sunday, off from Hagerstown. Destination Joliet, Illinois, where we RONed. Hazy all the way, but above minimums [meaning visibility was good enough to fly safely].

Seven WAFS at Hagerstown to pick up PT-26 closed-cockpit trainers: from left, Sis
Bernheim, Gertrude Meserve, Dorothy Fulton, Betty Gillies, Helen McGilvery, Teresa
James, and Nancy Batson *Courtesy: Robert Patterson, grandson of Colonel Robert H. Baker*

> *Up at 6 and out to the field. Took off. Landed first at Des*
> *Moines, followed by Grand Island, then North Platte,*
> *Nebraska, where we RONed. A beautiful afternoon. CAVU.**
> *Magnificent flying weather!*

---

*CAVU stands for ceiling and visibility unlimited. It means there are no
clouds above or below the aircraft, therefore visibility is unlimited.

Nancy Batson relished the trip. She later recalled, "It was green, like a shades-of-green patchwork quilt below. And by golly, we were headin' west in the cockpits of sleek new Army airplanes and somebody else was paying for the gas."

April 20, they were up at 4:30 and off at 7:25. Again, Betty wrote "CAVU" in her diary. "*And what scenery! Stopped at Scottsbluff AAB for gas, on to Casper, Wyoming. Delayed there two hours on account of weather at Billings, Montana—a front passing through. Finally it cleared and we were off for Billings. Gassed up there, then on to Great Falls, arriving 6:55. Total flying time today, 8 hour 15 minutes.*

"*A beautiful trip. Everything running smoothly. Knock on wood. Should deliver tomorrow.*"

On April 21 the WAFS delivered the PT-26s to the Royal Canadian Air Force flying school in Calgary. New York-born Sis Bernheim—this was her first trip west—was so impressed, she exclaimed to the others, "Did you see those mountains?"

Betty wrote: "*We caught a flight departing at 1:53 for Salt Lake City. A magnificent trip over breathtaking country. Weather CAVU. This was a never-to-be-forgotten-day! Someday I'm coming back to this country and thoroughly explore it. It's heavenly.*

"*The next day, spent a long day but restful, just sittin' in the airliner, watching the ground slide by. The pilot invited us up into the cockpit one at a time. We landed in Philadelphia and rode down to NCAAB in an airline limousine with 5 other pilots.*"

Back on base, Betty wrote: "*We have apparently set a record with our speedy trip to Calgary and Colonel Baker is tickled pink. He presented each of us with a wonderful letter of commendation. Then he sent a copy to Colonel Tunner in Cincinnati telling him about our Calgary delivery and praising us to the skies!*"

On April 27 Betty received orders she had been expecting. Six members of the first class to graduate from the flight training school in Houston, Texas, would report for duty May 9.

Betty walks toward a P-47 she is assigned to ferry. *Courtesy: WASP Archive, Texas Woman's University, Denton*

Chapter Eight

Betty's First P-47 Delivery

BETTY DIDN'T HAVE TO WAIT LONG for her first P-47 delivery assignment. The base C-60 transport flew her and several male pilots to Farmingdale, but when they arrived at the Republic factory, the aircraft weren't ready. Bad weather kept them grounded the next day, but on May 4 Betty made her first P-47 delivery.

"Off at 10:10. Destination Bedford Airdrome, Mass., 185 miles. Arrived over the field in fifty minutes. Mission completed! Ships delivered to the 359th Fighter Group. A big thrill. Toted my .45 'n' everything!

"I have delivered a P-47 and Helen Mary flew the '47 yesterday for the first time. She likes it!"

More good news: *"Colonel Baker says the WAFS can have the old Finance Building for our Alert Room.**

"It's going to be slick. Talked to the Red Cross about fixing it up for us, and they said they would. Also got some furniture from the quartermaster [officer in charge of supplies]."

As expected, on May 9 the six new WAFS arrived on base. Betty welcomed Dottie Young, Magda Tacke, Marion Mackey, Marjorie Gray, Jane Straughan, and Eleanor Boysen.

---

*This was a comfortable place to wait for assignment, also called a Ready Room.

The next day, the weather was beautiful. *"The new girls had their flight checks. They qualified on the PT-19, then flew the AT-6 this afternoon. A bull session in the BOQ this evening covered the fine points of ferrying."*

On May 15 Betty had the six new WAFS ready for the Saturday morning review. *"A Ceremonial Parade. It was quite a show!"*

A couple of days later, Helen Mary Clark flew her P-47 cross-country. *"She is all qualified to ferry! Away we go! I hope!"*

General George, Colonel Tunner, and the ATC had decided that the WAFS should be allowed to fly anything they could prove they were capable of flying. This was big! It meant the women pilots could climb the transition ladder and qualify to ferry bigger, faster aircraft including pursuit. Also, now all ferry pilots, male and female, would carry a card listing their classifications and the planes they were qualified to ferry.

On May 24 Colonel Baker approved the new policy allowing women to ferry the P-47. Immediately Betty and Helen Mary were placed on temporary duty at Farmingdale (FFM) on Long Island, the home of Republic Aviation. Their new job was to shuttle P-47s, most of them to the docks at Newark, New Jersey.

As more from Betty's squadron qualified in pursuit aircraft, they too would be allowed to ferry the big fighter.

The two left the next morning. *"Up to FFM in the C-60. Then Lt. Murphy led seven of us flying P-47s. Destination, take them to NCAAB. Then we went back to FFM in the C-60 to pick up seven more ships.*

"Took off, but this time we couldn't get into NCAAB on account of a heavy rainstorm. We were redirected to Philadelphia, where we circled for 25 minutes before landing. And there we stayed!"

Betty spent the night with relatives. She had no clean clothes, not even a toothbrush with her. Such was the life of an itinerant ferry pilot!

Betty and Helen Mary in Farmingdale for P-47 shuttle duty *Courtesy: The Gillies Family Collection*

"Today, it poured rain all morning, so we sat around the airport until it stopped. Then took off for NCAAB."

On May 27, *"Off for Farmingdale in the Cessna at 9:25—Helen Mary, Lt. Hook and me. Delivered three ships to Newark. Back to FFM. Took off again and delivered three more ships to Newark."*

The next day, *"Off for Newark again—three of us. Delivered. But we had to wait at Newark for the Cessna. It was late picking us up.*

Finally got back to the factory at 1:30. Then off again on the second delivery to Newark at 2:25—just Helen Mary and me this time. And that was all for the day.

"This time when I got back to FFM, I had a message from the base to return to New Castle. Tomorrow is NCAAB's First Anniversary celebration. Caught the 9 p.m. train." So ended Betty and Helen Mary's first extended stay at Farmingdale, specifically to ferry P-47s.

Nancy Love arrived the next morning for the big celebration, May 29, 1943.

"She, Colonel Baker and I had a good long talk before The Review took place. General George and staff and Colonel Tunner and staff all were on hand and it was quite something. Helen Mary and I were invited to join Nancy and the men to watch from the reviewing stand."

This was the Party of the Year. The NCAAB personnel marked their first year on the job. The men on base, the officers and staff, and the WAFS all celebrated a good and productive year. After the party, Esther Rathfelder left on maternity leave.

On June 1 Betty and Helen Mary again reported to the control officer at Republic for P-47 ferrying duty. Betty's dream for the future was to have a rotating squad of WAFS P-47 pilots in Farmingdale to shuttle aircraft to Newark. For now, Betty, Helen Mary, and a couple of the male pilots would be sent from NCAAB to shuttle P-47s as needed.

Chapter Nine

Cochran's Power Play

WITH THE FIRST GRADUATES from the women's flight training school scheduled to report to their Ferrying Division squadrons, Jackie Cochran put her plan in motion. She wanted command of all the women flying for the Army Air Forces. She sent the following memo to General Arnold:

> The more these women pilots are split up and spread around for operational purposes, the more need there is for overall coordination of problems common to them all, such as type of work to which they are assigned, promotions and discipline.
>
> You need eyes and ears in whom you have confidence, and they must be feminine. That's the job I would like to do, and which I think I can do well. You and I had this job in mind for myself from 1941 on.

ATC chief General George saw things differently. He wanted the women ferry pilots under the authority of the Ferrying Division Sector commander for whom they flew. Cochran disagreed with George. "He failed to distinguish between operational control and overall supervision of the women and general policies relating to them," she wrote.

Nancy Love delivers a B-25. *Courtesy: The Love Family Collection*

She told Arnold these young women needed a "woman's touch," and she was the woman to provide that touch. General Arnold gave her what she asked for.

✝ ✝ ✝

On June 14 Betty welcomed 10 members of the second Women's Flying Training Detachment class to graduate: Marie Muccie, Lila Chapman, Melvina Maier, Emily Hiester, Helen Stone, Mary Trotman, Rita Moynahan, Ruth Grimm, Virginia Alleman, and Catherine de Bernard. Betty got to work. She scheduled their flight checks and physical exams for the following day. Within two days, her new pilots finished their flight checks and were in ground school.

The Ferrying Division had been relocated to Cincinnati, Ohio, and Colonel Tunner wanted Nancy Love permanently stationed there. With the growing number of women in each squadron, he needed her to be his liaison as well as his trouble-shooter. By the end of June, 88 women made up the WAFS, and their numbers were increasing every few weeks as women graduated from the training school.

On June 25 Nancy Love and Long Beach–based WAFS Barbara Towne ferried a B-25 twin-engine bomber from the West Coast to Kansas City. This was a first for a woman pilot and copilot duo in a bomber. From there, Nancy went directly to Ferrying Division Headquarters in Cincinnati.

The Ferrying Division issued the following press release announcing Nancy's new assignment:

> Nancy Love has been appointed to the staff of Colonel William H. Tunner as Executive for WAFS. She will be stationed permanently in Cincinnati.
>
> Members of the WAFS are now flying any type of ship on which they can check out, including certain type bombers. The appointment of Mrs. Love is in recognition of this past achievement and the future importance of women ferry pilots.
>
> Undoubtedly this angle will make interesting material for articles on the WAFS in national publications as well as the fact that women ferry pilots are now flying the heavier type planes.

The WAFS were breaking military aviation barriers and making history. American women were flying combat aircraft. Sadly, the news media did not pick up on this news.

Betty was headed south again and, for once, it was a quick, uneventful trip.

"*Off in a '47—destination Tallahassee. Beautiful weather! Refueled Greensboro, landed Tallahassee. Total time 4 hours 30 minutes. Headed home. Caught an airliner to Jacksonville at 10:46. Sat until my next flight took off at 2:25 a.m."*

Back at NCAAB by mid-morning, Betty had just caught up on her paperwork when *"Jackie Cochran blew in. We had a long conflab* [an informal private conversation or discussion] *with Colonel Baker directing it."* Cochran exited as quickly as she had blown in.

The next day, Nancy Love flew into NCAAB. *"We had a long talk with Colonel Baker. Covered quite a bit of ground."* Odds are the three discussed this news.

The previous day, AAF Headquarters had named Jacqueline Cochran to the new position of Special Assistant and Director of Women Pilots in the Office of the Assistant Chief of Air Staff. The ATC and the Ferrying Division were not consulted, nor were they ever told what effect this appointment would have on the women ferry pilots.

"Nance is spending the night here, this time we really had a chance to talk, and we kept at it until midnight…" More than likely they discussed what the Cochran announcement would mean to the WAFS as a group and to them personally.

The next day, Betty was relieved to be sent to Farmingdale to ferry more P-47s.

"This morning, delayed by weather, but finally took off for Rome Air Depot in P-47. A swell trip, four of us ferrying aircraft. All of us back to FFM in the C-60. That was all for today, not enough time for another round trip."

Betty spent the Fourth of July at the Republic factory waiting for good weather. But it remained stormy all day. The P-47s sat on the runway, undelivered.

On July 5, the press announced Nancy Love's and Jackie Cochran's new appointments in separate press releases.

"The media exploited what it called a 'tussle for supremacy' between the two women," WAFS Del Scharr wrote in her memoir,

Teresa James flies the P-47. *Courtesy: WASP Archive, Texas Woman's University, Denton*

Sisters in the Sky. "*Newsweek*'s article was headlined 'Coup for Cochran: Last week came a shake up.'"

Author Marianne Verges wrote in *On Silver Wings*, "The newspapers and magazines played up the rivalry between Jackie and Nancy. They made Jackie's appointment seem like a victory in an ongoing war."

Cochran had no say in how the graduates of the Women's Flying Training Detachment were used once they were in the Ferry Command [another name for the Ferrying Division]. That didn't change. But the memorandum appeared to give her authority over all the women pilots.

Tunner and Cochran interpreted this announcement differently. Tunner considered Cochran to be an advisor to Air Staff. Her job was recruitment and training. However, Cochran took her new position quite seriously and prepared to act on her own interpretation of what the title meant.

Betty ignored the furor in the press. Her job was to see that the ferrying of aircraft by the women stationed with the 2nd Ferrying Group continued uninterrupted, other than by the unavoidable—the weather.

"*Good news!*" Betty wrote. "*Teresa James checked out on the P-47 today. Now three women are certified to ferry the P-47!*"

"*Today was a wonderful day. Four of us (three lieutenants and me) made five deliveries apiece to Newark. The Cessna picked us up each trip and everything clicked fine. Nine new pilots (male) came up from NCAAB this a.m. and they each made two trips to the Rome Air Depot in upstate New York, so the total deliveries out of Republic today was 38. A record!*"

Back at her desk at NCAAB the following day, Betty noted: "*Busy getting caught up. Helen Mary went up to FFM today with the new shuttle crew. Things are changing. She and I are going to alternate on the job. Colonel Baker wants one of us at NCAAB all the time.*"

Chapter Ten

"Something Big Is UP!"

COLONEL TUNNER WAS PROMOTED to brigadier general on July 12.

This morning, Colonel Baker received this Telex [a radio dispatch] from Cincinnati Hdqs: "Commanding General desires Mrs. Gillies be checked out on B-25 both day and night and that she be sent through instrument school at your group."—*It was signed Tunner!!! No other explanation.*

I talked to Major Matz and Captain McKay and got the ball rolling. McKay says I am to "sandbag" [build time on the airplane] *for a few hours on local transition. Suits me.*

In the alert room most of the day except for time spent sitting in a B-25 and in the Tech Order Room reading about it. Late this afternoon I "sandbagged" in a B-25 with Captain McKay and Lt. Perkins. We were out about an hour and I got a lot out of it. Quite an Airplane!

Two days later, "*Nancy Love blew in unexpectedly. She stayed overnight. We sat at the Officers' Club and talked long and hard.*"

On July 19 Betty was told to drop everything and go to Instrument School. Her B-25 transition was postponed for now.

She was back to flying under the hood, that black cotton cloth that obscures the pilot's vision outside the cockpit. With a safety pilot, she flew a single-engine BT-13 and then a twin-engine C-78.

The C-78 had varying propeller speeds, and landing gear and flaps that had to be manipulated on takeoff and landing, but Betty thought it was easier to fly under the hood than the BT-13. She wrote in her diary on July 20, "*Am gradually getting the feel of the ship. My trouble is with altitude, air speed and cockpit procedure. But I'm getting there!*"

On August 3, "*Got my Army Instrument Ticket!!* [certification] *Scored an average of 90 percent on the written. Starting back on the B-25 tomorrow.*"

Two days later, the WAFS received some unwelcome news. They learned that they had a new name: Women Airforce Service Pilots (WASP). The WAFS and Women's Flying Training Detachment were now under one name, and Jacqueline Cochran had been named director of the newly formed organization.

Betty's response was, "*We were WAFS until we woke up the morning of August 5 and learned that someone had changed our name while we slept! ALL WAFS WERE NOW WASP.*"

Betty was in for yet another surprise.

"*I AM TO REPORT CINCINNATI JUST AS SOON AS POSSIBLE!*

"*It was a mad dash to turn in papers, pack, shower, read mail. Departed noon. Nancy met me at the field and we had dinner.*"

That's when Betty learned why she had spent the past month in B-25 transition and Instrument School.

"*Nancy Love and I are to be checked out as pilot and copilot respectively in the four-engine B-17!*"

The next day, Nancy and Betty began cross-country training in the legendary B-17 bomber known as the Flying Fortress. Training would include night flying, night landings, instrument operations, and full operation of the aircraft under the careful tutelage and watchful eye of Captain Robert D. "Red" Forman, General Tunner's topmost instructor.

The B-17 Flying Fortress *Courtesy: National Museum of the U.S. Air Force*

On August 10 Betty recorded her first B-17 training flight in her diary. *"We started bright and early this morning. Flew over to Lockbourne AAB* [the B-17 training base at Columbus, Ohio] *and joined the B-17 traffic pattern there. What a sight! Dozens of them going round and round!*

"For awhile Captain Forman sat on the left and Nancy copiloted. Then she got on the left and Captain Forman copiloted. [The pilot-in-command sits in the left seat of the cockpit, and the copilot sits in the right seat.]

"I shot one landing late in the afternoon. My time: Right seat 2 hours. Left seat: 15 minutes with one landing. We stayed there until dark, coming back to Cincinnati in the moonlight and getting to bed about 11.

"Same thing the next day. Weather perfect! Sure do like the B-17!"

The next day, General Tunner called Nancy and Betty into his office. They were astounded to learn that they were going to ferry B-17s.

"Up at 5:45, out to the field and off for Lockbourne in the B-17. And there we stayed the rest of the day and most of the night. I got in 1 hour 15 minutes and nine landings in the left seat, 2½ hours copilot time, 55 minutes under the hood, followed by one landing and 1½ hours night flying (six more landings).

"My night landings were better than my day landings! We didn't get back to Cincinnati until 1:30 a.m. Captain Forman graduated us and declared us 'First Pilots' on B-17s. Tomorrow we start to deliver B-17s."

August 17, Nancy and Betty delivered their first Flying Fortress to the Modification Center at Cheyenne, Wyoming. With them was Technical Sergeant Hall who had flown with them throughout their transition and would serve as their crew chief on all their future deliveries.

The next morning, they delivered a modified B-17 to Great Falls, Montana. Then on to Seattle and Boeing Aircraft where the B-17s were built. There, they picked up another Fortress due for modification at Cheyenne. That one delivered, it was back to Seattle via airliner. Next was a delivery for Dallas, by way of Long Beach.

"Took off, but couldn't get through on account of weather. Went up to 12,000 feet, but a higher overcast soon merged with that below us. We didn't want to go on for fear of picking up ice in the clouds, so we came back to Seattle.

"Got to the hotel at 4:30 p.m.—our first opportunity to relax in a long time. Sent our pants out to be pressed and did some washing. I bought a tan sweater—it's cold up here!"

The next day, they landed in Long Beach. *"A grand reunion with BJ Erickson and Evelyn Sharp. First time I've seen them since they got transferred from NCAAB last January."*

Nancy and Betty get a look at their first B-17. *Courtesy: The Love Family Collection*

Next stop, El Paso. *"Under CAVU skies the entire flight. Stayed overnight at the Paso Del Norte Hotel. Had Mexican supper and got such a tummy ache I could hardly move. Clean hotel, wonderful bed.*

"Off for Dallas. Another beautiful morning. Delivered the ship to the Lockheed Modification Center. Spent the afternoon with the original WAFS stationed here—Florene Miller, Delphine Bohn, Betsy Ferguson, Helen Richards, and Dorothy Scott. It sure was a treat to see them all again. There are about fifty WASP stationed here and they have a slick set-up.

"And so ends our B-17 deliveries for the present."

August 25, Betty was back at NCAAB.

"Spent the evening talking to the girls and learning all that has happened in my absence. We have 20 new girls for a total of 52." The newcomers were the graduates of the fourth training class.

"Helen Mary is now in Instrument School."

The next morning: "*Busy as the dickens with all that has been going on in my long absence. Then at 5 p.m. I got a call from Nancy telling me that I am to go back to Cincinnati tomorrow for 30 days temporary duty!*

"*Then I really started rushing! Did my packing, washing, etc. and got caught up a bit at my desk.*"

Chapter Eleven

A B-17 Bound for England!

GENERAL TUNNER'S MALE PILOTS were complaining about ferrying B-17s across the North Atlantic to England. The weather was unpredictable with ice, fog, and poor visibility. Conditions were worse in the winter, which would arrive soon enough. The men considered the flight dangerous.

Tunner insisted, "Those flights have become almost routine." He saw no reason for complaint. The general had a solution to help the male pilots see it his way.

"Our women have proved themselves as ferry pilots," he wrote in his postwar memoir *Over the Hump*. "They pay attention in class, and they read the specifications of the plane they are to fly before they fly it. We'll let a couple of our girls show the men just how easy it is to ferry a B-17 across the Atlantic to England."

Tunner called Nancy Love into his office. "We've scheduled a blitz movement of two hundred B-17s," he told his top woman pilot. "They're to be delivered to the Eighth Air Force in England in early September. I want you and Mrs. Gillies to fly one of them."

Nancy Love and Betty Gillies leapt at the chance to be the first U.S. women to ferry a four-engine aircraft overseas in wartime.

September 1, 1943: Nancy, Betty, and crew took off for Presque Isle, Maine, in a B-17 christened "Queen Bee." Presque Isle was the first stopping point for flights across the North Atlantic.

"Hit CAVU weather about 20 miles south of Presque Isle and landed at 1:58. RON.

"Gathered at the base commander's home, with Crocker Snow* and many others. — Dinner followed. General Tunner also arrived this afternoon!" The men of the Ferrying Division had gathered in Presque Isle to send their two favorite ladies off to England in style.

The next morning, Nancy, Betty, and their crew flew northeast for Goose Bay, Labrador, their last stop before crossing the North Atlantic. "A fascinating trip. Three hours over wilderness! There we found a perfectly beautiful airport—one of the finest I have ever seen.

"The Air Base is unbelievable. Briefings at 5—subject, the trip tomorrow to Bluie West One (BW1) in Greenland. [The base in Greenland was their next destination.] Spent the night at the hotel, which was very comfortable, in fact luxurious!"

On September 5 the crew remained in place due to bad weather in Greenland. Betty's diary describes what happened next: "At Goose the weather was lovely. We were treated to a sightseeing flight around the area. In fact, we had a wonderful day—up until dinner!

"In the midst of eating fresh salmon, the blow fell.

"A radio message arrived from General Arnold cancelling our flight to England and recalling us. A male pilot and copilot were being sent to take our ship on! Our B-17 was going to England without us. That was a war zone."

General Arnold's message read: "Just have seen message from C.R. Smith … indicating that a B-17 with women crew will leave for England shortly … Desire that this trip be cancelled and no women fly transoceanic planes until I have had time to study and approve."

Disappointed only begins to describe how Nancy and Betty felt the following morning as they boarded a flight headed back to the States.

---

*Crocker Snow, an old friend of Nancy Love's and a veteran pilot, was in charge of construction of USAAF's North Atlantic sector airports.

A disappointed Betty and Nancy get a last look at "their ship," Queen Bee, before it heads for Scotland without them. *Courtesy: WASP Archive, Texas Woman's University, Denton*

They'd been replaced by two male pilots who delivered the Queen Bee to the Eighth Air Force in Prestwick, Scotland. Betty and Nancy made the best of it, but they were not happy.

*Off in a C-54. With us, an adorable Eskimo puppy, 3
months old, which I purchased from a Sgt. about 15 minutes
before departure. His name is "DeGink" and he is precious!*

*When we changed to American Airlines in Boston, we had
to smuggle DeGink aboard as no dogs allowed, but got away
with it OK. He rode in Nancy's duffle bag! Nance went on to
Washington. Bud met me at La Guardia and we drove home.
The kids were thrilled with DeGink. He behaved perfectly. I
am so glad I got him!*

In defense of General Tunner's decision, General C. R. Smith, deputy
commander of the Air Transport Command, wrote to chief of the Air
Staff Major General Barney M. Giles on September 7. Here are excerpts:

The Ferrying Division/Air Transport Command (FD/ATC)
considered the flight to be routine.

Because it WAS unusual for two female pilots to "arrive in any
country in a B-17 bomber," the ATC thought it should be one of
them—not someone else—that notified General Arnold that the
flight was taking place.

U.S. women were serving as ferry pilots, and their eventual use
as ferry pilots to "foreign destinations" was a strong possibility.

"Both Mrs. Gillies and Mrs. Love are capable pilots with far greater experience than the average male pilot taking a B-17 across the
ocean." They were well trained and capable of performing the job.

Smith reminded Giles that he had, in fact, told him over lunch
that the ATC planned to send its women fliers across the ocean
when they felt the women were ready.

Smith believed that Nancy and Betty's assignment should go
forward. "There are plenty of B-17s to go across and this is a capable crew." And he added that they should go "before the weather
over the North Atlantic gets too bad."

But they never had another opportunity.

Chapter Twelve

Big Changes Ahead

BETTY RETURNED TO NCAAB just in time for a formal review in honor of Colonel Baker. Her friend and staunch supporter had been named to command the Central Section of the Ferrying Division. It was a big promotion, but it meant a move. He was on his way to Kansas City.

"*Sure hate to see Colonel Baker go!*" Betty wrote, then she added, "*About 30 WASP present for the review—we looked good!*"

Betty's absence from base the prior two weeks meant that the 20 new women from the Training Command had not yet been through transition. Some reorganization was in order. "*Trying to stir up transition for the new gals. Think I got somewhere!*"

Betty needed to complete her postponed B-25 transition. She scheduled a flight the following afternoon. That night she reported in her diary, "*Jackie Cochran blew in for a visit. I was scheduled to fly the B-25, so I left in the middle of the discussion.*"

Cochran was there to tell the women on base that they would be getting WASP uniforms. This news was greeted with enthusiasm by the girls from the training school. At that time only the original WAFS had official uniforms. The WAFS loved their gray uniforms and wore them with pride. But new blue uniforms were in the works.

Betty gladly welcomed Esther Manning Rathfelder back the following day. Esther's maternity leave was over. She left her three-month-old baby boy in the care of her parents and a nanny, and returned to the WASP squadron. She was ready to resume her job as Betty's administrative assistant and to ferry as needed.

Betty was delighted and relieved. Esther couldn't have picked a better time, because the next day Betty learned that 34 new girls would arrive later in September. They were graduates of the fifth training school class.

Word of five minor accidents by women graduates of the Texas flight training school had alarmed General Tunner. Concerned that they had not had sufficient training, he released the five women from ferrying duty. Immediately, he ordered a significant upgrading of the school's training curriculum.

Cochran called in the air inspector (an independent investigator who was part of the AAF command staff) and demanded an inquiry.

Betty and all the women who flew for Tunner, and respected him and his policies, were upset by Cochran's actions. The FD/ATC complained that she was interfering with his command.

Colonel Oliver La Farge, ATC historian, wrote in *The Eagle in the Egg*: "There was a steady push and pull between the ATC and Miss Cochran over the clash between [ATC's] sole desire to get on with its mission of delivering aircraft and training pilots and her [desire] to conduct a large experiment." Cochran's goal was "implementing her concept of a special corps of women pilots ... flying for the Army Air Forces."

The inquiry's finding, based on the inspector flying with several trainees and graduates, was that, generally, the women trainees were adequate pilots. The problem was, Tunner wanted far better than "adequate." But he had to back off and let the upgraded instruction at the WASP training center, now located in Sweetwater, Texas, do its job. After the sixth class graduated that October, no more graduates were to be sent to the Ferrying Division until Sweetwater produced pilots with considerably more training.

The direction of the war had changed. The Allies, playing defense until now, had gone on the offensive. The AAF no longer needed more small planes to train pilots. The big push now was for warplanes—fighters and bombers. The production of trainers slowed to a crawl, and the manufacture of pursuit-type aircraft was fast-tracked.

The Ferrying Division had two new missions. The top priority now was to qualify male pilots to fly four-engine bombers overseas. The second priority was to train more pilots to ferry fighter aircraft, also known as pursuits. Those aircraft needed to be flown from the factories to the docks to be shipped abroad to the war zones. The more women who could qualify to ferry pursuits, the more male pilots could be sent to overseas duty.

Tunner and his staff had discovered that learning to fly single-engine pursuit aircraft could be omitted from four-engine aircraft training. "Although these fast, powerful aircraft certainly required more than average experience, the flying of fighters was not in itself of great experience value in working up to the big four-engine planes," Tunner wrote.

Why waste time and money teaching male pilots to fly single-engine pursuits when it added nothing to advance their bomber training? General Arnold had forbidden the women to fly overseas. Why not let them do as much of the pursuit ferrying as possible inside the United States?

The Ferrying Division no longer needed women to ferry trainers. They would have to be assigned elsewhere, and Jackie Cochran already was working to find the new women pilots other assignments. But those WASP who could learn to ferry pursuit aircraft had a slot waiting for them in the Ferrying Division.

Tunner knew that his WASP pilots could fly pursuits. By August 1943, seven of the original WAFS were ferrying them: Betty Gillies, Nancy Love, BJ Erickson, Teresa James, Helen Mary Clark, Del Scharr, and Evelyn Sharp. Two others, Barbara Donahue and Gertrude Meserve, had made their first pursuit flights.

The Ferrying Division now had 180 WASP ferry pilots on active duty. Of those, 64 of them were on track to qualify for pursuit training, provided a facility could be made available to train them. Eight were original WAFS and 56 were early graduates of the training school.

A Pursuit School was about to become a reality.

Chapter Thirteen

Betty Flies the P-51

SEPTEMBER 22: *"This morning an SOS came in for ALL P-47 pilots—*
a blitz movement from Farmingdale to the Republic modification center
in Evansville, Indiana. Helen Mary is still in Instrument School. I gave
them Teresa's name and mine."

Two WAFS and every available NCAAB male P-47 pilot headed immediately for Farmingdale. There, they all took off for
Evansville where the P-47s they delivered would be modified
according to where in the various war zones they were being sent.

Teresa and Betty expected to be sent back to Farmingdale that
night. Instead, they were sent west.

"The Control Officer at the Mod Center asked us if we would like to take
two P-47s on out to California!! Needless to say, we were delighted. He called
NCAAB and told Group Operations that he was using two of their pilots—
namely Gillies and James—for a priority movement to Long Beach!!"

Weather delayed them all along the route. Six days later they
delivered to Long Beach. *"We sold our airplanes at the Long Beach*
Sub Depot, then reported to Group Operations for further orders."

Betty and Teresa were in for yet another surprise.

"Our further orders are to check out in P-51 Mustangs and take
them east!" Betty and Teresa reported to Transition and were put on
the schedule to be checked out on the P-51 the next day. They
stayed overnight at the WAFS BOQ.

public Aviation News — Indiana Division   October 15, 1943

First Woman Ever to Fly a Thunderbolt Is One of Two Girls Landing Here in P-47's

Betty Gillies, WAFS Pal Bring in Two, Take Two

IT WAS just routine, of course, when a pair of P-47's dropped out of the eastern sky the other day and landed at the Modification Center.

And it caused only a ripple of concern when the pilot that climbed out of one was a goodlooking girl.

But Raider interest and individual temperature gauges rose with a start when another tiny mite of a woman casually piled out of the other Thunderbolt. And fever heat hit the top of the tube when "the little one" turned out to be none other than Mrs. Betty Gillies, who about a year ago became the first woman ever to fly a Republic Thunderbolt.

Flew P-47's for Months

Betty and Miss Thresa James, the other girl pilot, are members of the Women's Auxiliary Ferrying Squadron and came in from the New Castle Army Air base at Wilmington, Del. They have been flying P-47's for many months in the East, from the Farmingdale plant, but it was their first trip to the Indiana Division.

Betty is just five feet one inch in height and it is hard to imagine that she has been doing the "man sized" job of ferrying 13,000 pound Thunderbolts, capable of over 400 m.p.h., all over the country. Besides that, however, she was the first pilot to qualify for the WAFS. At present Betty is the squadron leader of the WAFS in the Second Ferrying Group at Wilmington.

Message for Raiders

Thresa is also one of this original group of WAFS which included 25 women, all professional fliers before the war. She is a native of Pittsburgh, Pa., and has some 2,800 flying hours to her credit. Both girls are members of the "99," an international club of women flyers formed by Amelia Earhart, and Betty was president of the club for two years.

They left Evansville airport the next afternoon, both flying new Thunderbolts, (which they praised as "a sweet plane") for delivery at a West Coast air base.

"Everyone here in Evansville seems so nice, we want to come back soon," Betty said. Thresa added, "Tell those Raiders at Republic to keep those Thunderbolts rollin' off the line. We can't fly them to where they'll do some good until we get 'em."

On October 1 both qualified in the P-51. Each was assigned a Mustang to take to a Fighter Group in Florida. Late afternoon they took off for Palm Springs, a short hop over San Gorgonio Pass between the San Bernardino and the San Jacinto Mountains. RON Palm Springs.

"Feel a bit strange in the P-51 due to so little time in it, but like it a lot," Betty wrote in her diary.

Early the next morning, they headed east. Encountering bad weather all across Texas, the trip took four days. They delivered to

Teresa James, left, and Betty Gillies deliver two P-47s to the Republic Aviation modification center in Evansville, Indiana *Courtesy: The Gillies Family Collection*

the 54th Fighter Group at Bartow, Florida, on October 5. Teresa was given a P-47 to take back west. Betty headed home to NCAAB. Her P-51 flight was the first of many to come.

Betty had very good news waiting for her when she returned to NCAAB. Helen Richey was coming to fly for the 2nd Ferrying Group.

Richey was an aviation legend. In the 1930s she was a barnstormer, a stunt flyer, champion race pilot, and the holder of speed, altitude, and endurance records. She was the first female Air Mail pilot and the first woman to fly a scheduled airliner. And she was Amelia Earhart's copilot in the cross-country Bendix Air Race in 1936, the first time women were allowed to enter. They placed fifth.

Helen Richey *Courtesy: WASP Archive, Texas Woman's University, Denton*

Helen was among the 25 American women Jackie Cochran took to England in the spring of 1942 to ferry aircraft for the British Air Transport Authority (ATA). There, Helen had flown the British Spitfire pursuit and many other high-powered aircraft. When Cochran left England to return to the United States in September 1942, she put Helen in charge of the American contingent of ATA women in Britain.

When her mother became seriously ill in December 1942, Helen felt she needed to return home and handed in her resignation. But Helen missed flying and grew restless after a few weeks at home. Late in January 1943, she applied for the WAFS.

The problem was, as of January 26, the option to qualify for the WAFS had been closed by General Arnold. Helen's interview and examination should have been a mere formality. But instead of sending her to a ferrying squadron—for which she was exceptionally qualified—Cochran sent her to the flight training school. Helen became part of the fifth class at the school in Sweetwater. There, she trained with women who had 35 hours, a drop in the bucket compared to her extensive experience.

When Helen graduated in late September 1943, she was assigned to the 2nd Ferrying Group. Betty was absolutely delighted.

Dorothy Scott *Courtesy: Scott Family Collection*

Chapter Fourteen

The Pot Boils

BACK AT NCAAB after her P-47/P-51 trip, Betty called on the 14 new members of the sixth class from the Texas flight training school. She welcomed them to the WASP squadron of the 2nd Ferrying Group.

On October 23 Betty was offered a flight in an OA-14, a twin-engine amphibious aircraft (it lands on water or on land). *"That's a Widgeon! Would I!"* she noted in her diary that night.

The Widgeon was built by Grumman Aircraft, the company Betty's husband, Bud, worked for. She had flown what the Army now called the OA-14 many times and was quite fond of it.

This Widgeon's destination was the Gunnery School in Harlingen, Texas. On the final leg of her flight there, Betty delighted in flying along the Gulf Coast via Corpus Christi to Harlingen. *"The ceiling was about 1200 feet, so I had to fly low and could see everything! Weather hot! Ship delivered at 7:50 p.m. RON Harlingen."*

She caught the noon flight to Dallas the next day. *"Had two hours to kill, so I called over to the 5th Ferrying Group. Dorothy Scott came over to spend the time with me."*

Dorothy, WAFS number 25, had proved to be an outstanding pilot. She went to Dallas with Nancy Love and three others in January 1943 to establish the women's ferrying squadron with the 5th Ferrying Group there.

Like all the other WAFS, Dorothy loved to fly and her passion for flying was contagious. But Betty found a different Dorothy that October afternoon. The young woman was grounded with a bad sinus infection. That's why she was on base that day. All the other women were out delivering aircraft.

This nagging infection threatened to put Dorothy on permanent non-flying status. Potentially, it could end her flying career. Flying, to Dorothy, was everything. She had been badly in need of someone to talk to. Her best friend, WAFS Helen Richards, had been transferred to Long Beach, and Betsy Ferguson, the other WAFS close to Dorothy, was on medical leave.

Then who should happen to fly into Dallas with a couple of hours to kill but Betty Gillies. From her time in Wilmington, Dorothy knew Betty was a good listener, and she took advantage of the opportunity to speak freely.

In addition to her personal health qualms, Dorothy also was concerned about the conflict in the Dallas squadron that had followed the temporary elimination of the five women in September and by the subsequent arrival of the air inspector at Dallas.

After the five women sent telegrams to Cochran complaining about transition at Dallas, Nancy Love had appointed Dorothy her liaison to the women arriving from the Training Command. Dorothy was well liked. She was friendly and enthusiastic and worked well with other people. Nancy needed someone like that to greet the new arrivals from the training school, talk to them, and help them feel at home.

Dorothy had written home that she thought her work as liaison to the new girls was paying off. She also wrote that she disliked the politics and second-guessing that sometimes plagued the Dallas squadron.*

---

*Dorothy Scott's letters written home during her ferrying service are the basis for this author's book about her, *Finding Dorothy Scott: Letters of a WASP Pilot.* The letters are held in the WASP Archive at Texas Woman's University.

Now rumors were flying about who from the squadron was going to Pursuit School. Nancy Love had told Dorothy, personally, that she was going, but Dorothy didn't know who else had been assigned. She knew that some of the girls didn't want to go and was concerned how that would affect the squadron.

After her conversation with Betty, Dorothy wrote the following to Nancy Love, telling of her concerns:

The way I see it is that you get all the "official" information and I get some of the undercurrent gossip, so if I tell you what I learn it might help you out. Darn if I like to appear as a stool pigeon, but if you don't know some of this stuff and should, this is OK.

Following their long talk, Dorothy saw Betty off at 7:45 that evening.

Betty had learned a good bit about the Dallas squadron from Dorothy, but all she wrote in her diary later that night was, "*We went for a ride in her car and she talked hard and fast.*"

Back at NCAAB the next day, Betty threw herself into her squadron work. "*Helen Richey and I had a long-planned bull session.*"

Nancy Love was back at NCAAB the following day. Betty wrote:

> *Helen Mary, Helen Richey and I went in to meet her train and we all had another long, healthy bull session over dinner at the DuPont Hotel. Back to BOQ about 11, we continued the session until about 1 a.m. Nance is spending the night here.*
>
> *Helen Mary and I decided to go down to Washington with Nancy to see what we could do! We three met our WAC Captain friends for dinner. We had a very interesting discussion as to how we might get Jackie Cochran out of office.*

Betty, Helen Mary, and the original WAFS as a group wanted desperately to do something about Cochran's interference with the work of the Ferrying Division and its women ferry pilots. They knew the job they were doing was vital. Where they were headed now—Pursuit School and pursuit delivery—was critical to the war effort.

In Washington, D.C., Betty and Helen Mary met with a succession of AAF officers they hoped would listen and help.

"We had quite a session and we told ALL! Don't know how much good it will do, but we got a lot off our chests and sure put it in the right place—the Operations Commitments and Requirements officer under which Cochran works!"

Chapter Fifteen

Will the WASP Be Militarized?

CONGRESSMAN JOHN COSTELLO of California introduced a bill in Congress in fall 1943 calling for the militarization of the WASP.

Why militarize the women pilots? Their lack of military status was a form of discrimination against them because of what they did not have as civilian employees. Military status would give them military insurance, death benefits, hospitalization insurance, and pensions. And their WASP service would be a matter of record for postwar government employment.

Cochran and General Arnold favored the Costello Bill. The women ferry pilots did not oppose militarization, but most of them opposed serving under Cochran.

Pursuit School opened in Palm Springs on December 1, 1943. Three of Betty's WAFS—Nancy Batson, Helen McGilvery, and Gertrude Meserve—reported for training. Four other WAFS also entered training in December: Dorothy Scott and Florene Miller from Dallas, Barbara Donahue from Romulus, and Helen Richards from Long Beach.

On December 4 Betty left Farmingdale to deliver a P-47 to Long Beach. Darkness caught up with her, and she had to RON at

NCAAB. There, she was shocked and saddened to learn that Dorothy Scott, with whom she had spent those two hours in Dallas a month earlier, had been killed in a crash at Pursuit School.

During a landing sequence on December 3, another student pilot—unable to see Dorothy's plane because of the late afternoon glare—had come in over the top of her aircraft. They collided in midair over the runway. All three pilots died: Dorothy and her instructor and the pilot of the other plane. The tower had failed to alert either pilot, therefore bore the blame for the accident. [See Author's Note on Pages 177-178 for more about Dorothy.]

Nancy Love had now lost two from her original WAFS squadron.

Betty took off the following morning in the P-47, destination Atlanta. The weather kept her in Atlanta for two days, followed by three days' delay in Shreveport, and two more days in Midland, Texas. In Midland, she found 200 more westbound airplanes, all flown by Army and Navy ferry pilots, grounded by the weather.

"When Guadalupe Pass, 5,424 feet in elevation between Midland and El Paso, finally opened, there was a wild scramble. Only one poor guy to sign weather clearances and a handful of linemen to get all the ships started. It was something!"

Betty landed in Long Beach on December 14 and RONed there. Already, she had been gone from base 10 days.

"Went in to call on Long Beach C.O. Colonel Cannon first thing this a.m. and he said how would I like to take a P-38 back?

"Would I!"

Nancy Love had flown the P-38 Lightning (a twin-engine pursuit/fighter) for the first time just two weeks earlier. Now it was Betty's turn.

"He called Transition and got me started. Had a cockpit check then studied the tech orders, filled out the questionnaire and got to fly it for an hour and 45 minutes this afternoon. Only got in 2 landings. The battery and generator were bad.

"Got put on orders to deliver to Newark and will shoot a couple of landings before departure tomorrow. Sure like the ship, it lands itself!"

Once again Betty's rudder blocks had worked their magic. "If I'd had to put enough cushions behind me to reach the rudders on the P-38, my nose would have smashed right into the gun panel."

Her orders and the P-38's official papers in hand, Betty took off the next morning. Two days later she wrote, "Landed Newark just before dark! Mission Complete! Whew! Caught the Red Cross Motor Corps transportation to the Railroad Station and the train to Wilmington. Arriving NCAAB 11 p.m. And so ends an all-around interesting trip!"

Back at her desk the following morning, Betty spent the day getting caught up. By then, she had been gone from base for 15 days.

On December 23 Betty let most of her girls go home for Christmas, with orders to return Sunday night, December 26. "Good deal!! Holding six on alert for a possible PT trip tomorrow."

But no PT orders came through.

December 24: "Group Ops said I could let all the girls go until Monday a.m. So off they went, leaving just a skeleton office force and three girls in Instrument School. So peace reigns here. I departed NCAAB for home at 3:30 p.m., by train, leaving everything under control."

Chapter Sixteen

A Valiant Effort

JANUARY 3, 1944: *"Esther Rathfelder and I left this afternoon to attend the WASP Squadron leaders and Operations Officers meeting in Cincinnati. Took the train on account of weather, left Wilmington at 6."*

Attending were: Barbara Erickson and Bea Medes from Long Beach; Delphine Bohn and Avanell Pinckley from Dallas; Lenore McElroy and Margaret Ann Hamilton, Romulus; Betty and Esther from NCAAB; and of course Nancy Love. Barbara Donahue, Romulus squadron leader, was in Pursuit School at Palm Springs, so her second-in-command McElroy and Operations Officer Hamilton attended in her place.

Betty very much favored the three suggestions under consideration. Using WASP as copilots in twin- and four-engine aircraft would give the women additional training and hours of experience. She also supported sending potential pursuit pilots to St. Joseph, Missouri, for instrument training. And she was for alternating four girls "in charge" at each base instead of two. With four sharing responsibilities, all the women could fly more.

After dinner together at a hotel, the group spent the rest of the evening in off-the-record discussion.

January 6, Betty wrote: *"ATC's biggest need is for us to fly the single-engine pursuits as well as twin-engine P-38s, A-20s and A-30s. We are setting up our training program with that in mind."*

Barbara "BJ" Erickson *Courtesy: Barbara Erickson*
London Family Collection

Then she added: *"The subject of militarization has been painfully avoided! Off the record, BJ, Delphine, Esther and I are going to Washington to see what's what! We got orders for BJ and Delphine to proceed to NCAAB 'to coordinate WASP affairs'. Leaving Cincinnati tomorrow a.m! Planning to delay in Washington en route."*

Esther Rathfelder, who also kept a diary, wrote this about the January 6 meeting:

> So far nothing new is startling Betty, like the suggestion that the girls who don't want to fly pursuits should be stopped at Class II transition [small twin-engine]. That was Betty's idea to begin with.

Delphine Bohn *Courtesy: Scott Family Collection*

This morning was mostly a rehash of things we've been discussing at Wilmington for weeks plus gripes from the other bases, all of which made us feel disgustingly smug. As for militarization, Nancy is truly on the spot in this.

As she said at dinner tonight, she can't quit even if militarized under J.C. and still make a decent return for all the good things ATC has done for her. And, of course, being a lady she cannot meet J.C. on her own ground.

On January 7, Betty noted in her diary, *"We decided to go see Jackie Cochran and feel her out. Spent about two hours in her office and got nowhere. But it was an interesting experiment."*

BJ Erickson had decided to apply for an Army commission with a Service Pilot's rating. This is how male Service Pilots were hired. The WASP ferry pilots were performing the same duties as the men at the ferrying bases. The only difference was that, after 90 days, the male pilots received Army commissions.

Betty, BJ, and the others searched Army regulations for anything that might prohibit a woman ferry pilot from being commissioned in the Army. They found no reason they could not join the Army as Service Pilots. On January 8, Betty visited the Navy Bureau to inquire about the WASP ferrying for the Navy. She was told the Navy could and would use them. Then she went to see General Hall, AAF Deputy Chief of Staff at the Pentagon.

That night Betty wrote in her diary:

> *I managed to talk myself in to see him! When I asked him if it were possible for us to apply for and receive a Commission and a Service Pilot rating, he nearly jumped out of his chair. "By golly, if you can that solves all our problems!"*
>
> *He was most enthusiastic and cooperative and said he would find out, and to please come back in a day or so!*
>
> *If we can go into the Army in this way, it will get us out of Cochran's clutches, and will need no legislation! We are officially going to be militarized, one way or another, and this is the way* **we** *want it done. So does General Hall.*

The four WAFS caught the 6 o'clock train to NCAAB. Betty, BJ, and Delphine spent the following day working up a proposed AAF regulation permitting them to apply for commissions as Service Pilots.

Betty wrote: *"We checked all the regulations and can find no snags! We even talked it over with two of the officers here. They approved of our efforts and plans. We are going back down to Washington tomorrow and present our efforts to General Hall!"*

BJ, Delphine, and Betty caught the 10:40 a.m. train to Washington Monday morning. They called General Hall on arrival, and he told them to come right over.

"He sure is a peach!" Betty wrote. *"Things look very promising! He seems to approve of our ideas and wants them to work out as much as we do! As yet he has not been able to find out if there are any snags, but told us to call him in a day or so."*

BJ and Delphine were so encouraged at that point, both called their home bases and asked for unofficial permission to remain in Washington for a couple more days. Permission was granted.

That night Betty wrote: *"I left them there to keep in touch with the general and caught the 6 o'clock train back to NCAAB."*

Unfortunately for Betty and the other squadron leaders, their hopes were dashed. The reply two days later said that nothing was found giving "authority" to commission women as officers in the Army. Where today's women likely would have pushed back, in the 1940s such action was rare. Besides, though civilians, they were under military command.

The effort made by Betty and the other three who traveled to Washington that January, though well thought out and valiant on behalf of the women ferry pilots, was doomed to failure. Now Betty and the other squadron commanders knew what Nancy Love already knew. If the WASP were militarized, they would be under the command of Colonel Jacqueline Cochran. It was unavoidable.

They weren't happy, but they were stuck with it.

Many years later, BJ Erickson London said in an interview: "Jackie wanted equal status with WAC Colonel Oveta Culp Hobby and the other women commanders of military units. She needed the thousand-member WASP in order for that to happen."

Thus the necessity for Jackie to keep all the women ferry pilots under her authority.

"Nancy Love thought that Jackie's influence was unbeatable— her wealthy husband, both President Franklin Roosevelt and First Lady Eleanor, General Arnold. Nancy had made up her mind," BJ continued. "She thought Cochran could bring it [the militarization] off."

Chapter Seventeen

Mid-Winter Blues

JANUARY 30, EN ROUTE TO LONG BEACH in a P-47, Betty once again was stuck in Shreveport, Louisiana. It felt like a repeat of the 15-day-long December trip. *"Am at Barksdale Field along with about 100 other Army & Navy ships. Weather socked in ahead."*

Betty was dreading a long, dull layover but happened to bump into three pilots she knew. *"Had dinner with three Marines I met recently at a Christmas gathering back home. Swell boys. We went to the movies after dinner. Saw a lousy show, but had a lot of fun. Interesting guys!"*

The next morning, *"Waiting for clearance—exhausting! Finally flight control said it was OK to go, so there was a mad scramble. I got off at 2 in the afternoon."* Betty delivered to Long Beach February 4. She RONed at the WASP quarters.

"This a.m. I went in to pay my respects to Colonel Cannon. He asked what I would like to take back and I said an A-20!

"He said, 'why sure' and called Transition for me. I put in 2-3 hours of local flying in an A-20 this morning and like it fine! Got the necessary forms filled out and the orders to take that particular A-20 to the mod center at Daggett, California, a short trip."

Betty delivered the A-20 to Daggett at 3:30 and was promptly assigned a modified A-20 to take east to Memphis. It was too late in the day to head east, so the control officer told Betty to RON there.

A-20 Havoc *Courtesy: National Museum of the U.S. Air Force*

That night, Betty wrote: "*An amazing place, a mod center run by Douglas Aircraft way out in the desert! Quite a city of barracks for civilian employees. Had a nice room in one of the barracks. Went bicycle riding in the moonlight with some of the boys tonight. Lots of fun! Wonderful place for cycling.*"

When the ceiling cleared in the morning, Betty took off for Memphis, stopping for gas at Winslow, Arizona. What came next was something that all ferry pilots dreaded—one of those rare moments of terror mixed into an otherwise normal, boringly calm and predictable day.

"*When I took off, my left outboard gas cap blew off! I had to go back and land! Lost 21 gallons in a brief circle of the field!!!*"

Though she had been in danger, Betty took it in stride. She noted in her diary that night: "*Off again, I landed at Albuquerque just at dark. Went into town and stayed at the Alvarado Hotel. Spent most of the evening in a hot bath! Gosh but it felt good!"* And she added some facts she had gathered from the day's trip. *"The A-20 cruises about 230 mph, using 155 gals per hour. Total gas aboard 500 gals."*

The next morning Betty flew to Amarillo. There, she learned that Wichita Falls and Memphis were closed. Oklahoma City was clear, so she headed there. Unfortunately, no hotel rooms were available, but resourceful Betty found a place to sleep.

"RON OKC tonight finds me sleeping in the OCADO* Hotel, right in the middle of a Hangar, with a B-29 [four-engine bomber] *on my right and a C-47 and a C-46* [two twin-engine cargo/transport planes] *on my left. Amazing!"*

Her "bed" was an army cot.

The next day: *"Delivered the A-20 to the C.O. at Memphis late this morning,"* Betty wrote. *"Sat around all afternoon trying to catch a ride home, but no luck. Finally gave up and went over to the Airline Terminal where I had afternoon tea and supper. Killed time until my flight departed at 11:30. A long wait!*

"Didn't do much sleeping last night, though it was a good smooth ride. Got off at Baltimore at 7 a.m. and caught the 7:43 train for Wilmington—getting to NCAAB and the office about 9:30.

"Spent the rest of the day getting caught up. Long talks of woe from many sources, but nothing that can't be fixed."

This time, Betty had been gone from base for almost two weeks. Such was the unpredictable life of a ferry pilot.

✝ ✝ ✝

In mid-March Betty and several WASP were ordered to Farmingdale on the P-47 shuttle. Fresh snow fell overnight. By then, Batson, McGilvery, and Meserve, as well as Emily Hiester and

---

*OCADO is believed to stand for the Oklahoma City Air Defense Operation. During WWII, the 404th P-47 Fighter Wing was located there.

Jane Straughan, had returned from Pursuit School. They joined Betty, Helen Mary, and Teresa flying P-47s to Newark.

"Runways were full of slush and snow, but the weather was CAVU. We each made one trip over to Newark. Runways there equally bad. The C-60 came over and brought us back from Newark to FFM to pick up more ships, but none were ready."

Rain and fog the next day, no flying. Group Ops asked Betty to return to NCAAB. Five new girls had reported from Sweetwater.

The women were graduates of the 10th training school class, the first to be assigned to Betty since October. General Tunner's upgraded flight instruction program at Sweetwater had paid off. Betty found that these new graduates had benefited from the improved program of instruction.

That evening, she wrote, *"Late afternoon, I had a long talk with Colonel McLaughlin on matters pertaining to transition and the future of the WASP at this base. Sure do miss Colonel Baker. I feel that the colonel isn't very much in favor of WASP. However I'm glad I talked to him today. I laid all my cards on the table and got a lot off my chest."*

The future of her squadron and all the women of the Ferry Command was, at that point, of great concern to Betty.

Chapter Eighteen

Changes Coming

AS OF JANUARY 1944, the war had turned fully in the favor of the Allies. General Arnold had enough pilots. Now the United States needed not more pilots, but more foot soldiers, ground troops, the walking army.

Arnold shut down the training program that had been giving future combat pilots their primary flight instruction. The male pilots who had been giving that flight instruction promptly lost their jobs. They complained to Congress. Then the AAF released the men scheduled for aircrew training from their obligation, meaning those men, too, were now eligible for the walking army.

At the same time, General Arnold was ready to militarize the WASP. The House Armed Services Committee scheduled hearings on the bill to militarize the WASP. They began March 22 in Washington. Jackie Cochran, her assistant Ethel Sheehy, and Nancy Love, all dressed in their new blue WASP uniforms, sat in attendance as General Arnold testified.

The general urged passage of the WASP bill, citing the shortage of manpower in the Army. He wanted to use the WASP as full military personnel for noncombat service—to replace men with women wherever possible. This would free more men for overseas duty.

The Committee recommended the bill for passage and sent it back to Congress to be scheduled for a vote.

Those men now eligible to be drafted to serve as foot soldiers fought back. They all complained to Congress and, with the help of a willing press, they began to take it out on the WASP.

Then, Congress's Civil Service Investigating Committee announced an inquiry into whether the WASP program should be continued since so many experienced male pilots were looking for jobs. (In the 1940s, it was commonly accepted that women didn't "need" to work.)

On April 1 Betty got word that she needed to be in Cincinnati the following day for a meeting of WASP squadron leaders. She boarded the westbound train for Cincinnati at midnight and arrived the following evening for dinner with Nancy and the others.

April 3, "*In session all day. Had a brief meeting with General Tunner. Planning to move a lot of girls out of the 2nd and the 6th Ferrying Groups and to start new squadrons at Palm Springs and Kansas City. Dinner later in Nancy's room. Went to bed about 1:30.*"

Pursuit School was being moved from Palm Springs to Brownsville, Texas. Palm Springs was needed to serve as a pursuit ferrying base.

At the bottom of that page in her diary, in small cramped handwriting, is this note that Betty added later: "*Evelyn Sharp was killed today in a P-38 at Harrisburg, Pennsylvania. One engine failed on take-off. A terrific tragedy and a great loss to us all. Her first P-38 trip.*"

Nancy Love had now lost her third original WAFS. BJ Erickson, Evelyn's squadron leader and close friend, was in Cincinnati for the meeting. She was stunned, as were all the others. Evelyn, one of her closest friends, was well liked and was a superb pilot.*

---

*See Author's Note on Pages 177-178 for more about Evelyn.

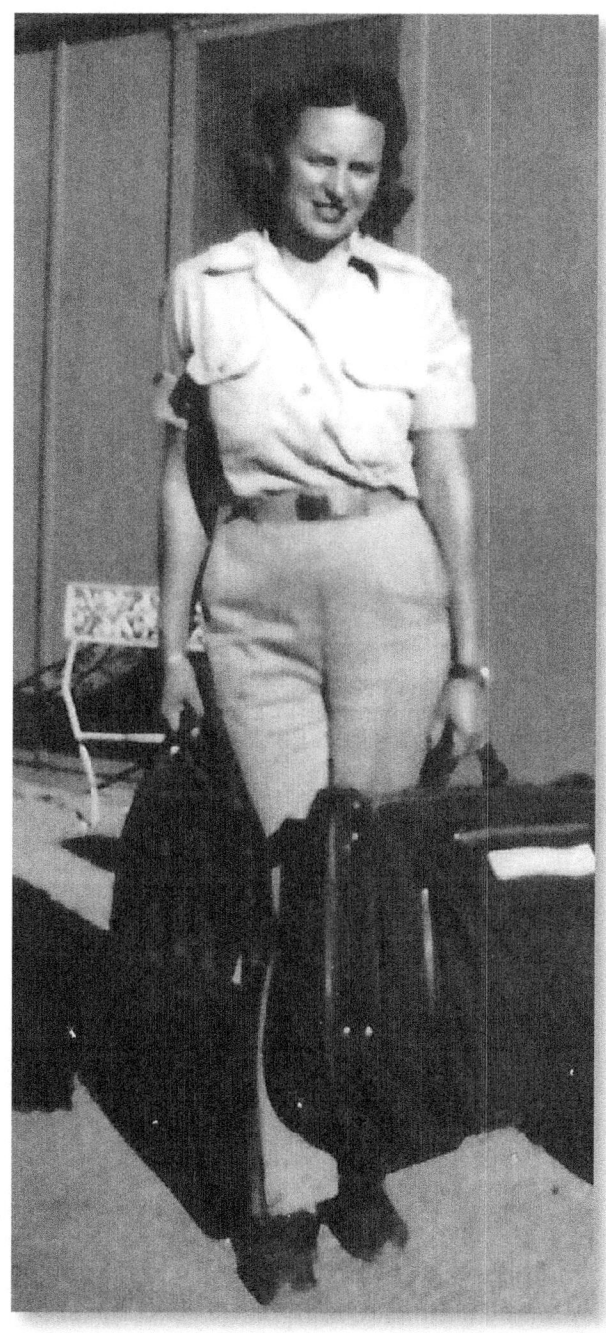

Evelyn Sharp *Courtesy: WASP Archive, Texas Woman's University, Denton*

The following morning, Betty was not surprised to learn that she needed to move 40 of her pilots out of NCAAB. The women were Class II pilots, qualified only in single-engine and small twin-engine trainer-type aircraft. BJ Erickson received similar orders for Long Beach.

Only pursuit-qualified women, or those expected to qualify soon for Pursuit School, were to remain in the WASP ferrying squadrons.

Nancy Love appointed Helen Richey to form and lead the new squadron in Kansas City. The women sent there were to serve as copilots ferrying twin-engine B-25s, built nearby. This was to help them build time in the bigger twin-engine aircraft in order to qualify for Pursuit School.

Betty hated to lose Helen, but her friend had earned the squadron leader's job.

Back at NCAAB, Betty and Esther Rathfelder spent the next day planning their transfers. WASP who were good candidates for Pursuit School were sent to Palm Springs, which was due to become a pursuit-only base. Five went to Dallas and five to Romulus—both still had small aircraft to ferry—and 24 were assigned to Kansas City to fly for Helen Richey's new squadron.

"That leaves 40 here," Betty wrote. *"Seven will go to instrument training in St. Joe; four to pursuit training at the new location, Brownsville, Texas; and six to Officer Training School in Orlando, Florida.*

"Richey got in from Long Beach this afternoon," Betty wrote the following day. *"Much confusion over all the transfers. A complete mad house! All 40 girls clearing at about the same time."*

Colonel Coates came in from Cincinnati to talk to Betty about the new congressional Civil Service investigation that was looking into WASP training at Sweetwater. Congressman Robert Ramspeck of Georgia had been appointed chair of the committee investigating the Army's need for the WASP.

The issue was heating up. How much were the WASP costing the government? Coates told Betty to expect a call from the Ramspeck Committee.

"It's a political mess in Washington," Betty wrote in her diary that evening.

The afternoon of April 13, Betty did receive a phone call from Mr. Shillito, the chief investigator for the Ramspeck Committee. They had a long conversation.

That night Betty wrote: *"He's investigating the WASP situation for the House Rules Committee. Mr. Shillito thinks the WASP bill will be killed! Seems to know the whole situation—all about J.C.*

"After dinner had a large bull session at the Club with Rathfelder, Richey and Batson."

Chapter Nineteen

Officer Training School

ARMY AIR FORCES (AAF) HEADQUARTERS thought WASP militarization would be a shoo-in once the revised Costello Bill went to Congress. Jackie Cochran moved to prepare the WASP to receive commissions in the AAF.

A March 27, 1944, letter to each WASP explained why she was being sent to Officer Training School: "As Women Airforce Service Pilots are becoming an integral part of the Army Air Forces it is desired that all WASP personnel be given training similar to that for Army Air Forces officers."

Officer Training School, or OTS (the formal title was The School of Applied Tactics), was located in Orlando, Florida. The women were selected in order of the length of time they had served.

Betty was due in Orlando for OTS on Wednesday, April 19. She had stopped writing in her diary. Best guess is, she stopped writing because everything caught up with her in those days as she was busy trying to transfer girls and to get ready for OTS. She could catch up later.

WAFS Nancy Love, BJ Erickson, Del Scharr, Florene Miller, Barbara Donahue, Delphine Bohn, and Betty, all past or present squadron commanders, were in Orlando. Also attending was Nancy Batson, recently returned from her trip to Ord, Nebraska, escorting Evelyn Sharp's body home for burial.

The gang at Officer Training in Orlando: Front row, Betty Gillies, Nancy Batson;
Second row, Delphine Bohn, Nancy Love, Jill McCormick, and in front of Jill, Shirley
Ingalls; Third row, Cappy Vail, BJ Erickson, Claire Callaghan. Fourth row, Barbara
Donahue, just above her, Florene Miller. The other three unidentified. *Author's personal
collection, gift from Nancy Batson Crews*

Betty and Batson may have been the two who got the most out of OTS because both talked in glowing terms about the experience.

"We attended class six days a week, studying military discipline, courtesy and customs," Batson said. "We also learned about the organization of the army and staff procedures. We were learning how to be officers. Besides, it was the first time some of us original WAFS had been together in more than a year."

The WASP had many visitors while they were in Orlando. Columnists and reporters bothered them with prying questions about dating. And they wanted to know things like "how do you keep your makeup looking fresh while flying? How do you manage to put on your lipstick?"

The WASP realized the reporters had no clue as to what they really were doing for the war effort.

Robert Ramspeck also came to talk to them. Delphine Bohn described his visit in her memoir: "He invited Nancy Love and three or four of us to have dinner with him. All the while he queried us about the WASP. He was experienced in this type research. He brought with him newspapers containing many columnist's opinions as to the WASP programs."

The women attending OTS were expected to be officers in the Army Air Forces, and they were treated just like the male officer candidates. Maids kept the barracks, did their laundry, and polished their shoes. The women had never been treated so well.

From a public relations point of view, the timing couldn't have been worse. The congressional hearings were being held, and their fate was being debated across the country. Now here were those very women being granted a four-week training session (critics called it a vacation) to make them officers, yet their militarization was in question.

Because of their busy ferrying schedules on their respective bases, the women ferry pilots hadn't had much leave or leisure time over the course of their months of active service.

Now, the Ferrying Division desperately needed every pursuit ferry pilot it had, male and female. Those aircraft needed to be moved. The loss of the women pursuit pilots for four weeks meant a lot of badly needed fighters didn't get delivered. Though it wasn't publicly known, D-Day—the Allies' planned troop landings on the French coast—was just over a month away.

Betty returned to writing in her diary on May 5, recording a 45-minute ride in the high-altitude chamber at 38,000 feet. *"Have never had a more interesting experience. Had no trouble whatsoever. Thank Goodness!*

"Into town for dinner with the gang. Katherine Rawls Thompson, a WAFS who left a year ago, flew up from Miami to spend the night."

May 12 was Diploma Day. Nancy Love logged the highest score, and Betty was second. *"My average for the course was 94.4. Not bad! So ends our session. Sure did enjoy it! Dinner at the Officers Club with the gang, then packed."*

Back at NCAAB May 15, Betty wrote: *"Esther Rathfelder got back from Pursuit School this morning—she washed out. Marjorie Gray also washed out. Tough."*

The next day Betty received a most welcome call from Cincinnati. *"We are going to have a WASP Fighter Squadron here and nothing else!"*

The job of ferrying P-47s from the factory in Farmingdale to Newark, to the mod center at Evansville, or to anywhere else in the United States now belonged exclusively to Betty and her WASP squadron.

"We will have to transfer all the girls out of here who are not checked out on pursuit! But this suits me—it's what I have always wanted! Farmingdale for our very own!"

Betty had her dream squadron and her dream command.

Chapter Twenty

A WASP-Only Squadron

D-DAY JUNE 6: The women at Farmingdale, like the rest of the world, celebrated the landing of American and Allied troops on the beaches at Normandy, France. The fight to free Europe from German occupation had begun. Betty logged three P-47 deliveries to Newark that day and five the next day.

On June 8, Betty and her all-woman squadron delivered three P-47s each. They repeated that effort the following day.

Betty now had 14 pursuit-qualified WASP pilots at NCAAB: six original WAFS—Nancy Batson, Helen Mary Clark, Helen McGilvery, Gertrude Meserve, Teresa James, and herself; six Houston graduates—Virginia Alleman, Emily Hiester, Rita Moynahan, Esther Poole, Jane Straughan, and Ruth Grimm Trees; and two Sweetwater graduates—Dorothy Colburn and Tex Clair.

More were on their way. By early July, Ruth Anderson, Celia Hunter, Jo Pitz, Mary Russo, and Mary C. Wilson had graduated from Pursuit School and joined them, for a total of 19 pursuit pilots. On July 15, original WAFS Sis Bernheim graduated from Pursuit School and rejoined the squadron, bringing the number to 20.

Now, every Thunderbolt that came off the Republic Aviation assembly line in Farmingdale was delivered to Newark, or wherever it was going, by a woman pilot.

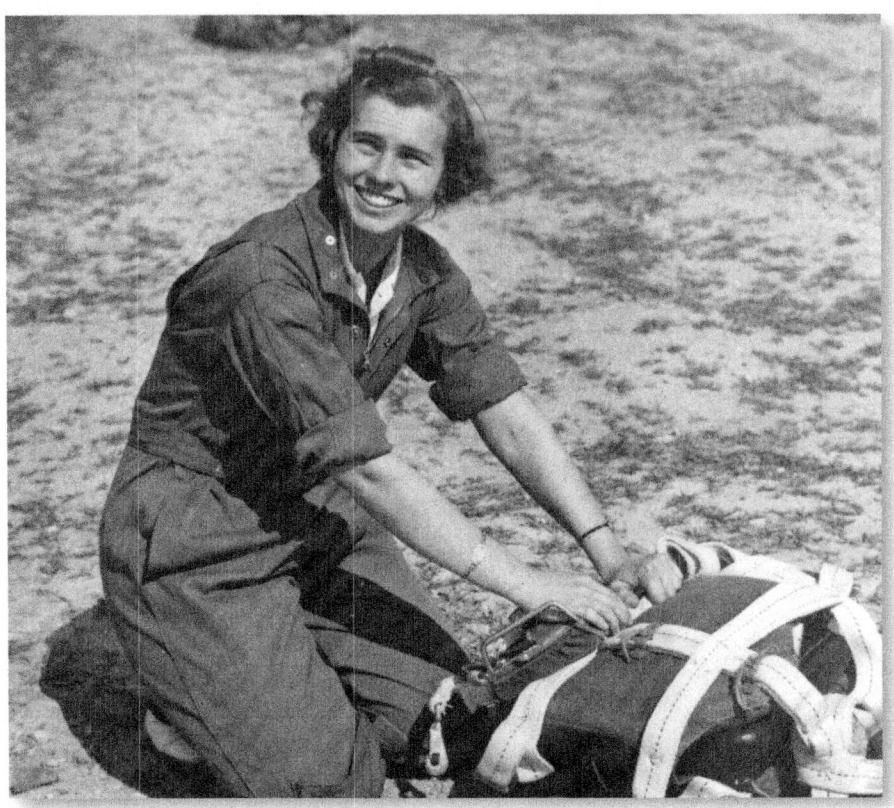

Gertrude Meserve *Courtesy: WASP Archive, Texas Woman's University, Denton*

Back at NCAAB, Betty had orders to pick up a P-51D at Charlotte, North Carolina, and bring it back to Newark. A male pilot flew Betty to Charlotte to pick up her P-51D.

"The temperature was over 100 degrees! When I got my ship started, I discovered the coolant temperature gauge was out. It was Sunday so nobody was working at the Sub Depo. RON Charlotte. Stayed at the Women's Club on base, dinner at the Officer's Club and went to the movies. I nearly melted!!!"

Once the coolant temp gauge was fixed the following morning, Betty took off.

"Good weather as far as Washington, then ran into a huge line squall [a line of thunderstorms forming along or ahead of a cold front].

Flew parallel to it, trying to get to Newcastle, but was pushed south. Finally landed at Dover [Delaware]. Storm hit 10 minutes later. It was a humdinger!

"*The boys took me to lunch at the Officers Mess and it was fun. Finally, off for NCAAB. Waited an hour there until Newark opened up, then took off and delivered the ship. Took the 6:45 train for Wilmington.*

"*Talked to Helen Stone most of the evening. She was eliminated at pursuit school.*"

While Betty and her WASP pilots were busy delivering P-47s, the fate of the WASP wasn't faring so well in Washington. On June 5—the day before D-Day—the long-awaited Ramspeck Report was released. Paraphrased, it said:

The WASP program was "costly and unnecessary." It recruited inexperienced young women.

It made possible the "dismissing of/failing to utilize" male instructors.

It lowered standards for women while keeping them high for men.*

The program was experimental.

Using women to alleviate the "claimed" manpower shortage was not working.

The committee recommended that Congress shut down the flight training program but retain WASP already actively serving, and that those in training at Sweetwater be allowed to complete the course.

Until then, Congress had given Hap Arnold anything he asked for to fight the war against Germany and Japan, but things had changed. Anti-WASP militarization groups lobbied Congress, and the press ran derogatory stories about them.

---

*The FD/ATC did not lower its standards other than when ordered to do so by the commanding general. Cochran, on the other hand, lowered standards when it served her purpose.

Major U.S. newspapers like the *New York Times*, the *New York Herald Tribune*, and the *Boston Globe* supported the WASP.

"Unfortunately, many other newspapers sided with the civilian male pilots and with others claiming the WASP held jobs men should have," Author Sally VanWagenen Keil wrote in her book *Those Wonderful Women in Their Flying Machines*. "The WASP program was called everything from a 'blunder' to a 'fast play' to a 'racket'. One wrote, 'Wanted Female-Impersonators.' Another referred to them as 'Jackie Cochran's glamour girls.' 'How about some of these 35-hour female wonders swapping their flying togs for nurses' uniforms?' wrote another."

AAF Headquarters asked General George for comments. George asked General Tunner to compile a report detailing WASP performance on the job. "Make it thorough and make it good," he emphasized.

Tunner sought input from his Ferrying Group commanders. He knew they would give him straightforward answers.

A few outspoken male pilots did resent the WASP, the men reported, but the supervisory and operational personnel, whose sole interest was the efficient operation of the ferrying mission, did not share this resentment. "Those personnel are familiar with the pilot shortage in the Ferrying Division and appreciate the WASP's contribution," they said.

What about the accusations of favoritism shown the WASP?

Tunner learned that WASP flying time averaged slightly less than that of male pilots. Ferrying missions were assigned to the pilot who had been on base the longest. Throughout the spring of 1944, the Ferrying Division had been overwhelmed with deliveries. All pilots, regardless of gender, were utilized without anyone waiting long for assignment.

Tunner's conclusion: "The WASP assisted in the performance of the Ferrying Division's mission when assistance was not available from any other source. During the past three-month period all Ferrying Division leaves had been cancelled due to a pilot shortage."

(The WASP's time spent at OTS was by military order, not for personal leave.)

General George presented the facts to the AAF to prove the naysayers wrong. Unfortunately, the ATC later determined that the report was NOT utilized by the AAF nor was it ever presented to the members of Congress.

Two weeks later, on June 21, the House Committee on Military Affairs sent the WASP bill to the House of Representatives for debate.

Congressman Costello, the sponsor of the bill and spokesman for the War Department, gave this very simple explanation of the bill.

> The sole purpose of this bill is simply this, to take
> these women who are now with the Army Air Forces
> in a civilian capacity and convert them into a military
> capacity. That is the sole purpose of the WASP bill,
> and nothing else.

The bill was doomed from the start. Congress, influenced by anti-WASP forces, had its mind made up. Representative Joseph O'Hara of Minnesota called it "social legislation to glamorize the war."

The Ramspeck Committee's recommendation was accepted, but the WASP bill died on the House floor.

Jacqueline Cochran wrote a final WASP report to General Arnold. She pointed out that by the time the WASP bill was defeated, Congress already had passed the Army Appropriations Bill, including $6 million in funds for the WASP program.

It didn't matter. By June 30, forty-eight women had reported to Sweetwater for the first class slated to graduate in 1945. Hasty arrangements were made to return them all to their homes. As ordered, the five classes currently in training at Sweetwater were allowed to finish, graduate, and be assigned to active duty.

P-61 Black Widow *Courtesy: National Museum of the U.S. Air Force*

Chapter Twenty-One

The Black Widow, P-61

BETTY DELIVERED A P-38 to Santa Maria, California, on June 30. In spite of her 2 a.m. arrival at the Long Beach WASP quarters—*"and a short night's sleep in a strange bed"*—Betty was up at 7.

She reported to crew assignment. *"'How would you like to take a P-61 to Sacramento?' says the Captain in charge.*

"Would I!!!

"So he writes me out an OK for P-61 transition and I go over to the school. Spent the a.m. studying Tech orders, filled out the questionnaire and this afternoon I got to fly one around the area for an hour. Liked the ship fine!"

That day, Betty Gillies become the first woman to fly the Army's new radar-equipped P-61 Northrop night fighter nicknamed the "Black Widow." The red light on top of the aircraft's black fuselage—part of the radar equipment—made it resemble the deadly spider by that name.

That night, with the flight east scheduled for the next day, Betty did what she did every night she was out on a ferrying trip. She sent Bud a telegram written in a code all their own. That night's message: *"Tomorrow, spinning a web to Sacramento."* Bud would know what she was flying, when, and where.

The following morning, after Long Beach's infamous morning fog had burned off, Betty spent two hours aloft to finish her checkout in the P-61.

"*Got my orders. I'm to deliver one to Sacramento. There, I'm to pick up another one for delivery to Newark!*" Betty took off that afternoon and delivered her first P-61. "*Beautiful trip! Ship delivered to Air Service Commander for Modifications, Sacramento. Stayed overnight in the Civilian Barracks.*"

Betty was off early the next morning in her second P-61. East of North Platte, Nebraska, she ran into a line of bad thunderstorms.

"*Found the way into Grand Island and made an emergency landing. The field was closed, the ceiling about 300 feet. The tower couldn't even see me on the runway! A terrific rain, so bad, it flooded the town. The staff car that picked me up got stuck in it on the way to the hotel, but we made it. RON Grand Island.*"

The next morning was clear, and Betty headed for Scott Field, Illinois. There, she gassed up and took off for Columbus, Ohio. Gassed up again, then on to Newark.

"*Completed mission at 9:05 p.m. Ship delivered! Total flying time from Sacramento, 11 hours 45 minutes. Good airplane! Train down to Wilmington, arriving at 11 p.m. Had a milk shake for dinner on the way out to the base. Talked to Batson 'til after midnight. Busy getting back to earth.*"

The next day, Betty was surprised to receive an urgent request for pilots to move Cubs. The government was selling off used aircraft that were no longer of use to the AAF. "*They are howling for pilots to move Cubs! OK, I'll go. Left Jo Pitz, who is temporarily grounded, in charge.*

"*Caught the 5 p.m. train to Washington. There I boarded a filthy, dismally packed train to Richmond. Got in after midnight. Couldn't find a room, so I called the OD [officer of the day] at the base and took a taxi out. I was put up in the WAC officers' quarters. Very comfortable. Got to bed about 2:15.*"

After breakfast with the WACs, Betty headed for Operations to pick up her Cub. "*Took off for Chincoteague Naval Air Station, 85 miles up the Atlantic coast. Gassed (5 gallons!!!) then on to NCAAB to RON.*

Betty's exclamation points—5 gallons!!!—emphasize how far the women flying for the Ferrying Division had come. Less than a week before, she had flown the Army's newest night fighter, the P-61, equipped with twin 2800-horsepower engines and a fuel capacity of 646 gallons. Today, she was moving a 60-horsepower Cub with an 11-gallon gas tank.

"Off at 8:20 for Reading, Pa, in my Cub. Mission completed. Spent most of the rest of the day trying to get back to NCAAB by train."

Nancy Love called from Cincinnati the following morning. She needed Betty to transfer 10 of her non-pursuit-qualified WASP back to the Training Command. *"Hated to do it 'cause now we need them to move Cubs—but orders is orders!"* Betty commented.

The demanding schedule continued. The next day Betty wrote, *"Would I please go over to Middletown and get two P-47s for delivery to Newark!"* She did. She delivered them both and was back at NCAAB in time for dinner.

Bad news caught up with Betty the next morning. *"Teresa James has gone home. Dink is missing in action. Damn tough!"*

Early in the war, before she became a WAFS, Teresa had married her flight student, George "Dink" Martin. Already famous in flying circles as "Teresa James, Girl Stunt Pilot," she never changed her last name. Dink, a B-17 pilot, had been sent to England the spring of 1944. Now his plane was down, and Dink was missing. Teresa went home to her family in Pittsburgh.

Chapter Twenty-Two

The Great Transfer

BETTY HAD GOTTEN TO KNOW TERESA pretty well by then. Two days later, she decided to call her. *"We need you Teresa. You know we're desperate for every pilot we can get."*

Teresa was never one to hide and lick her wounds, and by then, she'd had enough family sympathy and thinking time. "I'll be back tomorrow," she told Betty. And she was.

A week later, Teresa received Dink's last letter, written on June 21 and postmarked June 22, the day his plane was shot down. That was all Teresa would know for a very long time.

In an effort to get over the loss of her beloved Dink, Teresa threw herself into moving P-47s or flying any other aircraft Betty needed delivered. In spite of that, the WASP who knew her well—Betty, Nancy Batson, and the three Helens (McGilvery, Richey, and Clark)—described Teresa as a shadow of her former fun-loving self.

When Teresa still hadn't heard anything four months later, Helen Richey wrote to her good friend General Jimmy Doolittle. The leader of America's gutsy B-25 bombing raid on Tokyo, April 18, 1942, was now based in England. Helen thought he was in a position to ask the right questions. She asked him to check on Dink's disappearance for Teresa.

Doolittle learned that on June 22, sixteen days after D-Day, Dink's squadron took off on a raid over northern France. His plane was hit and had not returned to base, but nothing else was known. He was classified as missing on an operational mission.

After that, Teresa assumed Dink was a prisoner of war and that he would come home when the war was over. Then, in summer of 1945, she received a letter informing her that an official determination had been made of his death. But Teresa never gave up hope that Dink might come home.

In May 1984 she finally learned for sure that Dink had perished in the June 22, 1944, crash. Teresa visited the town in France where he was buried.

On July 16 Betty received an important Telex. She was needed in Detroit the next evening for a meeting of WASP squadron leaders. Betty was sure something big was brewing.

She was right. That same day, July 16, General George received a memo from AAF Headquarters: "A total of 126 WASP are to be transferred from the Air Transport Command back to the Flying Training Command." That meant nearly half of the WASP ferry pilots on duty no longer were needed to ferry aircraft, because they were not qualified on pursuit aircraft.

Betty arrived in time for dinner with the group. When Nancy met with Betty and her other squadron commanders in Romulus the following day, she passed the information on to them. The WASP, thereafter, referred to it as "the Great Transfer."

Betty wrote, "Again, we need to transfer Class 1 and 2 pilots out of the Ferrying Division. We will lose 12, leaving us 30 girls." At this point, approximately 100 WASP were delivering the bulk of America's new pursuit aircraft—most of them to Newark, New Jersey, to be shipped to England and the war in Europe.

"All of us had dinner at the Officers Club and talked on into the wee hours."

Betty caught the late train back to NCAAB.

Helen McGilvery climbs into a P-47. *Author's personal collection, courtesy Nancy Batson Crews*

Nancy Love also had received some welcome news in the form of a memo from Public Affairs. Subject: WASP Deliveries. The WASP had established a new record for completed movements of aircraft—953 for June 1944. Of those, 529 were pursuit deliveries, the most critical job now performed by the WASP of the Ferry Command.

So great was the demand for the P-51Ds that pursuit pilots stationed near the factories producing P-51s (Long Beach and Dallas) ferried little else. When a WASP arrived back on base before noon, she was sent right back out that afternoon. Otherwise, she was sent out the following day.

The strain was beginning to tell. The end of July, back from deliveries to and from Long Beach, Betty found an ailing Esther Rathfelder.

"Esther is very sick," Betty wrote in her diary July 29. *"I got her to the hospital this morning. The diagnosis is bronchial pneumonia!"* Esther was going to be out of commission for some time.

"Helen Mary and Teresa are in Orlando at OTS; Nancy Batson and seven others are working the Farmingdale Shuttle. Someone will have to be here and I guess that's me!" Betty wrote.

Esther wasn't the only one to fall ill. Betty's pursuit-qualified WASP were constantly busy moving P-47s from the factory in Farmingdale to Newark or Evansville. Already, several had been grounded for colds or other ailments. The strain was taking its toll. A few had taken short leaves in order to regain their health. Now a very sick Helen McGilvery had just gone home on medical leave. She, too, had pneumonia and would be away for a month.

Betty's pilots waiting for the Great Transfer were bored and restless because NCAAB no longer had aircraft they were qualified to ferry. But the date of their official transfer had not been set.

"Too many girls around—not busy enough," Betty wrote. She hoped, for their sakes, that they soon would be assigned to a base where their flying experience was needed and used. All were capable single- and small twin-engine pilots. They just weren't qualified to fly pursuit.

Chapter Twenty-Three

Summer and Strife, Both Heating Up

IN AUGUST BETTY WAS BACK in Shreveport again, but this time, instead of winter weather delays, she was dealing with heat, humidity, and a leaky coolant valve.

"Weather unbelievably hot and humid! I'm in Shreveport to pick up a P-51 to go to Newark, but the P-51 wasn't ready this morning. The generator was out.

"After an hour's delay, I finally took off for Nashville. There, the coolant boiled over while I was taxiing to the parking area. Two hours delay then off to Pittsburgh. Got within 80 miles, then had to turn back. Weather! Went to Columbus instead. That's where I am. RON."

The next morning, Betty found a puddle of coolant and a steady drip drip drip under her P-51.

"Five hours later the crew had located all four leaks and fixed them— by which time the weather east was not good enough to suit me. Low ceilings and thunderstorms. So RON Columbus again."

The next morning, the repairs were finally finished. Betty was anxious to get moving. The weather was marginal on the ground in Columbus, so she asked for—and received—a clearance for an "over the top" trip to Newark.

Betty relished flying up high, above the clouds, and she was well-schooled in it. She took off and flew at 13,000 feet. *"It was beautiful! One hour 15 minutes later, on the ground at Newark. Ship delivered!*

"Gee, I have fun! Sounds like a lot of trouble but I enjoy it!

"Back at NCAAB, I spent the evening talking to the girls. Many problems, as usual! Another flood of lousy articles in the newspapers has morale at a low ebb."

After the cancellation of additional WASP training at Sweetwater, Jackie Cochran drafted her report on the WASP for General Arnold. It was aimed at achieving militarization. She had not given up hope.

The press release date for the report was August 8. But influential columnist Drew Pearson broke the release date and published this sarcastic piece—"There Is Still Some Sting Left in the WASPs"—on August 6:

> Arnold's efforts to side-track the law by continuing to use the WASP while more than 5000 trained men pilots, each with an average of 1250 flying hours remain idle and hundreds of Air Corps pilots retiring from combat are anxious to stay in the Army as transport ferry pilots. ... Magnetic Miss Cochran seems to have quite a drag with the "brass hats."

Cochran's report, "Director of Women Pilots Asks Military Status for WASP," was an 11-page document with a two-page summary. She wrote a detailed account of the WASP of World War II. She had fashioned her concept of how to utilize women in several flying roles and then sold it to General Arnold. It was she who coined the name *WASP.*

She glossed over the WAFS beginnings, a model quite different from hers. She made no mention of General Tunner or Nancy Love or General George, whose foresight gave Love and Tunner the latitude to "go" with their concept of women's role in the Ferrying Division.

Cochran assumed all the credit for the accomplishments of the 1,102 women who flew for the WASP in World War II, and she made a solid case for their militarization.

Nancy Love's and Jackie Cochran's visions were very different.

Nancy had worked with the men of the Ferrying Division to prove the concept that the men and women should be under the same command, treated as the experienced pilots they were, judged on their capabilities, and allowed to transition into higher-performance aircraft as their skills permitted. Her argument was, the airplane doesn't "know" the gender of the pilot flying it.

Love had the full support and backing of the men she worked with in the Ferrying Division. Given her example and the record achieved by the women flying for her, Tunner and his men saw to it that male and female pilots were given the same opportunities for advancement—an early model for what exists in today's military.

Betty finally had good news about Esther. She was released from the hospital. "*She looks like the dickens and is now home on sick leave.*"

August 14, Betty received orders to transfer nine pilots back to the Training Command. Three of them resigned rather than transfer. Helen Stone, hearing that Cochran considered WASP who resigned to be ungrateful, wrote in her letter of resignation that she had come to the conclusion "that there are now far more pilots than are needed and so long as the shortage is over, it is time to resign."

Off on another California trip, Betty took a P-38 from Middletown, Pennsylvania, to Santa Rosa, California. With bad weather to the west, she decided to RON in Middletown and leave the next morning. Betty "bought" (signed the papers for) her airplane and gassed it up so she could get off early, which she did.

SNAFU Airlines: Betty with seven male pilots *Courtesy: The Gillies Family Collection*

This flight went well. "*Ship delivered! It was a P-38 training base!*

"*Had lunch with some of the boys, which was fun, then one of them flew me in a BT-13 down to Hamilton Field to catch the Long Beach shuttle. SNAFU* departed at 8:20. Slept most of the way to Long Beach but not very comfortably! Nearly 4 a.m. when I fell into bed at the WASP quarters.*"

Betty reported to Group Ops the next morning and was put on orders to take a P-38 to Newark. But there was a hitch. The aircraft was at Transition and couldn't be released until after 3.

---

*SNAFU Airlines, which stood for Situation Normal All Fouled Up, was the shuttle service at Long Beach. The shuttle flew ferry pilots to, or retrieved them from, remote delivery locations.

Betty wrote: "*While waiting had quite a talk with BJ Erickson and Iris Cummings.*"

Iris later recalled the August 20 conversation. "Betty had time to kill so she came over to talk to BJ. I was BJ's second in command and happened to be in the office. BJ asked me to stay.

"Betty had a lot on her mind—as did BJ, both being squadron commanders. This was the turning point for the WASP. We were aware of Cochran's dealings and that was the gist of the conversation."

The repercussions from Pearson's column and the many other articles related to Cochran's report were all over the news. The three discussed the demoralizing effect this was having on the women in BJ's and Betty's squadrons.

"It was evident we were reaching a crisis," Iris continued. "The end of the WASP was in sight and that was hard for all of us to take. The women pursuit pilots were still badly needed. We were busy every day.

"Both Betty and BJ were in the middle of sending some of their girls back to the Training Command. Several of them resigned rather than go elsewhere. They felt they were being thrown out with the trash. They had bought into Cochran's program and felt she had let them down."

Betty departed Long Beach Airport at 5:15 that afternoon and headed for Newark.

Chapter Twenty-Four

Betty Takes on Evansville

IN SEPTEMBER 1944 the ATC announced that the women ferry pilots were delivering three-fifths of the pursuit aircraft coming off the factory production lines.

Nancy Love was eager to place an auxiliary ferrying squadron at the Republic Aircraft modification center in Evansville, Indiana. From there, mid-continent America, WASP ferry pilots were in an excellent position to take the modified P-47s whatever direction they needed to go. Betty was to oversee that squadron in addition to her continuing responsibilities at NCAAB and Farmingdale.

Finally, the good news arrived from Cincinnati.

"The 'Evansville Deal' is under way. I'm to send four girls out there on TDY [temporary duty] next week. Hope it is the beginning of a beautiful friendship between Evansville and us.

"We'll have 16 girls stationed there, 10 at Farmingdale and the rest here at NCAAB for miscellaneous flying," Betty wrote. *"I have a few details to straighten out, but this should work well."*

Pursuit-qualified WASP from Romulus were being transferred to Betty, thus allowing her to staff and manage both Farmingdale and Evansville, as well as NCAAB. The P-63s the Romulus women had been ferrying weren't considered as critical to the war effort as were the P-47s. Also, Kansas City was closing down. Helen Richey was returning to NCAAB.

Jackie Cochran (second from left), Helen Dettweiler (her WASP assistant), and NCAAB pursuit ferry pilots Marianne Beard, Helen Richey, Gwen Cowart, Liz Pearce, Teresa James, (behind Teresa) Jo Pitz, Gertrude Meserve, and Betty Gillies attended the ceremony introducing Ten Grand, the 10,000th P-47 built at the Republic factory in Farmingdale. *Courtesy: International Women's Air and Space Museum, Cleveland, Ohio*

By mid-September 1944 Republic Aviation put out word that it was nearing production of its 10,000th P-47 Thunderbolt. The aircraft would bear the name Ten Grand.

The Army's first P-47 rolled off the line March 18, 1943. Five thousand employees made up the Republic workforce at that point. Now, 18 months later, 24,450 individuals—more than half of them women—were working at the Farmingdale plant. Production efficiency had improved as Republic strived to meet the Army's increased "road to victory" demands.

Production cost of Ten Grand, which rolled off the line September 20, 1944, was $45,000 (in 1944 dollars). The cost of the early P-47s built in 1943 had been $68,750 each.

Ready to follow Ten Grand out of the hangar: from left, Marianne Beard, Gertrude Meserve, Teresa James, Helen Richey, Betty Gillies, Captain Joe Tracy, Jackie Cochran, Albert Marchev, the president of Republic Aviation, Liz Pearce, Gwen Cowart, and Helen Dettweiler. *Courtesy: International Women's Air and Space Museum, Cleveland, Ohio*

And, making everything a little sweeter for the WASP and for the men and women at Republic Aviation, the Farmingdale division had just earned the War Department's Army/Navy Production Award for the third time. Republic was being thanked and praised for its efficiency.

Teresa James drew the "short straw" and was assigned to take Ten Grand on its first flight over to Newark. She recalled the day.

> Betty Gillies came up with the idea. She had a book of matches. She said, "Whoever comes up with the shortest takes the flight." She held them up and let each of us pick out the match we wanted. I wound up with the shortest one.

Everybody was there—Betty Gillies, Gertrude
Meserve, Helen Richey, all the other Farmingdale WASP,
and Captain Joe Tracy who had checked us WAFS out at
Wilmington back in '42.

Jackie Cochran had come in to christen the aircraft.
The crew rolled Ten Grand out the hangar door. They
pushed it up to where Jackie stood on a lift-truck platform,
holding a bottle of champagne. She smashed the bottle
on the propeller hub, then they moved the plane back.
    "That's when they beckoned to me to come forward.
I posed for a bunch of pictures, climbed into the cockpit
and they took a lot more pictures of me waving,"
Teresa said.

But because of bad weather, Teresa didn't actually fly Ten
Grand to Newark until September 22. "That's when I taxied that
big beauty over to the duty runway and—off we go into the wild
blue yonder. I was on my way to Newark. No cameras this time, but
it was a very big day."
    On September 23 a very pleased Betty Gillies wrote: "We deliv-
ered five ships apiece to Newark, making a total of 35 deliveries. Gertie
put in a full day toting us all back in the C-60. James flew P-47s over
and copiloted the C-60 with Gertie on the way back."
    Betty had plenty of reasons to be proud of her squadron.
    Then the ax fell.
    The night of October 3, Betty wrote this in her diary:
"Newspaper release today says WASP will be disbanded on Dec. 20th!
I called Nancy Love.
    "Nancy's tersely delivered words were: 'General Arnold so directs'."

General Arnold announced that the total casualties suffered by
the Army Air Forces since the outbreak of the war were far below

Teresa James taking off in Ten Grand *Author's personal collection, courtesy Teresa James*

the numbers anticipated. The AAF now had all the pilots it needed for present combat needs.

The WASP were expendable.

The women were stunned. They knew they were a vital part of the ongoing war effort. What they were doing was important. Six months earlier, Arnold had pleaded with Congress for their militarization because their country needed them badly!

The simple answer was: D-Day had been successful. Allied troops, after retaking Paris in August, were advancing on Germany. We were on the path to victory in Europe.

On October 8, all WASP received letters from Arnold and Cochran confirming the October 3 announcement.

The two letters arrived in the same envelope. Arnold's note was complimentary. But he concluded with this: "The situation is, that if you continue your service, you will be replacing instead of releasing our young men."

The WASP were not at all happy with that particular phrase.

And, author Sally VanWagenen Keil wrote, "As if Cochran knew the state of shock into which her readers would fall, her letter continued with an emotionless enumeration of details"—types of discharges, issue of civilian pilot ratings, final discharge physicals and logbook certifications, and more.

What mattered was, it was almost over.

Chapter Twenty-Five

A Last-Ditch Effort

ESTHER RATHFELDER, NOT COMPLETELY RECOVERED from her bout with pneumonia, resigned in mid-October. Marge Gray took over her duties, serving as Betty's right hand in the office. Helen Mary was now in command of the squadron in Evansville.

On October 17 Betty noted: *"The current crew at FFM: Batson and James on the C-60, Esther Poole, Ruth Adams, Liz Pearce, Nancy Baker, Emily Hiester and me on the P-47s. Good weather. Each of the gals got in two deliveries both days. Ships smooth as silk!"*

On October 31, looking ahead to the closing down of the WASP squadron at NCAAB, Betty returned and began gathering the group's statistics and committing them to the record. What she found was pretty impressive!

"It appears that in the past 10 months we have delivered 2,953 airplanes, of which 2,108 were pursuit types including eight A-20s, two P-61s and sixteen P-38s. All this was accomplished with an average available personnel of 34. Not bad!"

Betty doesn't say so, but she personally had delivered a good number of those A-20s and P-38s and both the P-61s.

On November 1 detailed instructions arrived for deactivating the women. Each WASP in good standing would receive a certificate of service and certification of pilot qualifications and horsepower rating.

Marge Gray *Courtesy: WASP Archive, Texas Woman's University, Denton*

General Robert E. Nowland, who had replaced General Tunner as commander of the Ferrying Division on August 1, made a last-ditch effort on behalf of the women ferry pilots. He sent this letter to General George.

> The cost of retraining male pilots to replace the WASP pursuit pilots upon their deactivation would be $9,336 per man. The total cost of training 117 men to replace the 117 women pursuit pilots leaving as of December 20, 1944, was calculated at $1,085,312.

General George passed Nowland's letter to Air Staff and seconded Nowland's position.

Jane Straughan *Courtesy: WASP Archive, Texas Woman's University, Denton*

"Richey went out to Evansville on the 6:10 train this morning," Betty noted on November 4. "Jane Straughan is off on a P-63 trip to Colorado Springs and Marge Gray is on orders to move two C-78s down in South Carolina. Sent Batson to Pittsburgh for a P-38 to go to Newark.

"That leaves me holding the fort alone at NCAAB."

Nancy Love flew into NCAAB the next day. She and Betty were overdue for a discussion on deactivation. They began the sad task of planning the WASP shut down.

"Nancy got off for Cincinnati in her A-20 this a.m. [By then, Nancy Love had an A-20 at her disposal for her trips to visit her squadrons.] I spent the morning in Operations figuring and figuring!

Nancy Batson and the P-38 she took from Pittsburgh to Newark in November 1944
Courtesy: WASP Archive, Texas Woman's University, Denton

This afternoon I spent in my room cleaning out drawers, going over my G.I. equipment. Am beginning to get ready to clear the post someday next month."

On November 6, *"Evansville called requesting P-47 pilots. Got Group Ops to agree to send two from FFM out to Evansville and let me take FFM. Everybody here is out except Gwen Cowart, who is grounded with a heck of a cold. I left her in charge."*

Betty was back in the office a couple of days later working on the files. *"What a mess! Threw out 3 baskets full of papers. Went over flight records, correcting discrepancies. Am trying to get things in shape for deactivation next month. Heck of a job."*

Air Staff's response to General Nowland's letter arrived November 22:

Inactivation of the WASP was based upon a policy decision, which has a vital effect upon the AAF as a whole. ... Evaluation of this program in terms of dollars and cents is not the immediate issue at stake and personnel under your control should scrupulously avoid any discussion along this line.

Thus, for the WASP, began the final unraveling of a dream.

Chapter Twenty-Six

"This Place Is Getting Me Down"

THOSE WERE BETTY'S EXACT WORDS in her November 17 diary post. She didn't like sitting in Wilmington.

November 18, *"There's an acute pilot shortage at Evansville due to weather holding up everybody enroute. Everything is caught up here, so, it makes sense for me to stop flying the desk and go back to flying airplanes!"*

Betty was up at 4:45 the next morning to catch the train to Washington. There, she took an airliner as far as Louisville. Bad weather in Louisville forced her to take the train the rest of the way to Evansville.

"5 hours to go 85 miles! Marianne Beard with me," Betty wrote later that night. Marianne was one of the WASP sent over from Romulus to ferry P-47s out of Evansville.

"We didn't get to Evansville until 8 p.m. Went out to the field to sign in then back to the WASP House. Quite a place, two stories, 16 cots, uppers and lowers; 3 baths; 2 kitchens; all very mixed up. Ruth Adams the only one here.

"I fell into a cot!"

November 21, Betty and Marianne took off in two P-47s; their destination was Oscoda, Michigan. They could clear only as far as South Bend, Indiana, where they landed in the middle of a snowstorm. They RONed in South Bend.

"*Weather still impossible today,*" Betty wrote that night, "*but we took off at 2 when it seemed to improve. Turned back to South Bend after 60 miles. Hit very heavy snow—ceiling about 300 feet, less than a mile visibility. Sure glad to put it back on the ground.*"

They delivered to Oscoda the next day. A B-17 flew them to Selfridge Field, north of Detroit. From there, a staff car took them on to Detroit where they RONed. There was no airline connection until 5 in the morning, so they sat. "*Finally made it back to Evansville in the middle of a pouring rain!*

"*Today, we got assigned a delivery to Selfridge, but couldn't get out on account of weather. When we got back to the house, we found Richey, Helen Mary, Pinckley, [Grace] Birge, Clair and Adams. So now we are a merry crew. Not enough hot water to go around!*

"*Weather today never did clear. Lots of airplanes ready to fly away at this point.*"

Finally, Betty and six others took off for Selfridge Field and, in spite of bad weather as far as Detroit, delivered their airplanes.

"*Visibility was down to one to two miles,*" Betty wrote. "*We had to fly at a thousand feet. At Selfridge, got a staff car back to Detroit City Airport and an airliner to Chicago. Three-and-a-half-hour layover there and finally to Evansville.*"

On November 30 Betty and Helen Richey received orders to take two P-47s to North Carolina. "*It finally cleared at 3:30, and we were able to get off! RON Nashville.*"

They delivered the following day. By this time every WASP was relishing every trip.

Back at NCAAB, Betty, Helen Mary, and Jane Straughan had a mission.

"*We three caught the 11:20 train to NYC,*" Betty wrote. "*Went straight to the New York Herald Tribune office.*"

They were there to see aviation expert and *Herald Tribune*

columnist Gill Robb Wilson but learned that he was detained in Washington. Wilson was getting information directly from ATC's second-in-command, General C. R. Smith.

The three were delighted and relieved to hear that he was getting an explanation of what was happening to the WASP from someone as in-the-know as Smith.

The women in Betty's squadron were fed up with the politics. Daily they performed the most important job ever given to them—helping win the war through their timely and devoted delivery of aircraft. And it was coming to a screeching halt, needlessly and prematurely, because the war was still on. Nevertheless, in two weeks, they would be dismissed and sent home, unless something happened to stop it.

"We plan now to meet Gill in Trenton [New Jersey] tomorrow morning. We caught the 8:30 train out of NYC for Trenton."

They found him open and willing to hear them out. *"Gill is as upset about all this as we are. He says all of ATC and Arnold's staff feels the same, but that Arnold is so far in he can't get out,"* Betty wrote.

"Gill is going to run a story in the Tribune."

In his December 13 column, Wilson criticized the AAF's waste of flying abilities brought on by the deactivation of the WASP of the Ferrying Division:

> Training men to take their places will require a million dollars, from four to six months time and even then will not replace the broad experience which the women have built up on pursuit-type aircraft. I just do not think the United States is rich enough to throw away two hundred* expert pilots, regardless of who they are.

---

*Actually there were fewer than 120 women ferrying pursuit by that time.

But the end of the war was in sight. Public opinion had turned against women "doing men's work," like flying military airplanes.

Betty finished her work on the files. When the squadron officially shut down, she would box them up and take them up to Central Files.

"I hope to go up to Farmingdale tomorrow and relieve some of the girls so that they can start clearing out. Only three of us on the post. They sure are keeping us busy up to the bitter end. Thank goodness!"

Chapter Twenty-Seven

D-for-Dismissal Day—
December 20

DECEMBER 14: "BACK UP TO FFM THIS A.M. *Delivered four P-47s, three of them the new M model. It's a swell airplane—2800 horsepower—gets off in almost half the distance the D model needs, climbs like the dickens and cruises about 20 mph faster. It's really a honey!*"

Betty delivered two more M models the next day. They turned out to be her last P-47 deliveries.

"*At the factory all day the 16th, but no deliveries to Newark. Weather! It started to snow about 3:30, so the lieutenant gave up for the day and told us we could go on down to NCAAB. Our big WASP Farewell party was scheduled for tonight.*"

"*We were flown down in the C-49. Landed about 6. Sure was disappointing not to get one last P-47M!*"

The WASP's private dinner—just the gals—was held in the Officers Mess at 8 o'clock. With mixed emotions, the women of the 2nd Ferrying Group's WASP squadron gathered for "The Last Supper," all smartly dressed in their blue WASP uniform jackets, skirts, and silver wings.

Nancy Love came from Ferrying Division Headquarters in Cincinnati to join the seven original WAFS still flying out of Wilmington. The eight of them occupied the head table, Betty and

"The Last Supper," New Castle AAB, December 16, 1944 *Author's personal collection, courtesy Nancy Batson Crews*

Nancy Love in the center. To Nancy's right were Nancy Batson, Helen McGilvery, and Gertrude Meserve. To Betty's left were her second-in-command Helen Mary Clark, Teresa James, and Sis Bernheim.

The eight friends were back where it all began. Joining the gathering was their housemother Mrs. Anderson (Andy). Thirty graduates of Houston and Sweetwater sat at tables down each side of the head table.

The menu was chicken à la king, sweet potato croquettes, fresh fruit, chocolate éclairs, and rare French wine to help with the toasts, which were sometimes long and often teary.

The WAFS laughed and reminisced about the "good old days" when it was just them in BOQ 14. The original eight remembered, with sorrow and regret, the three who did not survive their WAFS/WASP service: Cornelia Fort, Dorothy Scott, and Evelyn Sharp.

The evening was long and memorable. Neither Betty nor any of "her girls" present would ever forget it.

December 17: *"Spent this morning in the office. This afternoon began clearing the post."*

Bud had come down for the party that took place after the WASP's private dinner the evening before. He planned to take

The WASP Ferry Pilots, New Castle AAB, December 16, 1944. Betty Gillies and Nancy Love are in the center of the front row. Mrs. Anderson, back row far right. *Author's personal collection, courtesy Nancy Batson Crews*

home anything Betty did not need for her last few days at NCAAB. She would take the train home to Long Island when everything was wrapped up.

"Bud and I packed my stuff in the car. Really got a lot done. But no one else did! Have never seen so many knocked out gals!

"Operations called and wanted 14 pilots to move surplus PT-19s from Newark to Reddington, NJ, tomorrow. I was able to dig up only six, so had to put myself on the list. Seven of us will make two trips each."

On December 18 Betty and Bud were up at 5:15 a.m. They drove to Newark. Bud dropped Betty off at the airfield. The C-45 flew the other six up to Newark, and Betty met them there.

"The visibility was low but we finally got off in the PT-19s at 11:30. Landed at Reddington at noon. Ships delivered to Reconstruction Finance Corporation for sale.

"The C-45 picked us up and took us back to NK for the other seven ships and we were back at Reddington again by 2. All 14 PT-19s delivered

B. Allison "Bud" Gillies, Betty's husband *Courtesy: The Gillies Family Collection*

in one piece by Richey, Clark, Clair, [Betty] Scantland, Beard, Colburn and Gillies! Once again, the C-45 brought us back to NCAAB, and we were in BOQ 14 by 7 p.m."

The unspoken irony for the very game seven, all qualified pursuit pilots, was that they began and ended their WASP careers flying the same aircraft—the lowly PT-19, open cockpit, primary trainer.

December 19, the Day-Before-D-for-Dismissal Day.

"Needless to say, I was busy today!" Betty wrote that evening. *"In the office all day. Did find time to do a bit of 'clearing the post' myself. Some of the girls left today. Gosh it is sad to watch the whole thing break up. The last eight girls came down from Farmingdale tonight!"*

Later that night, the unthinkable happened!

Very early the morning of December 20, Betty wrote this:

"The Officers Club burned down tonight. It caught fire shortly after midnight and burned all the way to the ground. The flames were terrific and the wind blew the sparks right at BOQ 14. Just in case, we dressed and packed and waited 'til it was safe to retire—about 3 a.m."

Nancy Batson was one of the pilots who had come back from Farmingdale that evening. Wearing her coat over her bathrobe, she joined the crowd outside in the cold. Together, the remaining WASP watched as the O-Club went down in flames.

Years later, Nancy recalled for this author the thoughts that crossed her mind as she watched the building burn. She felt she was watching her future burn along with the O-Club, the fixture that had been their after-hours retreat following a long day of flying.

Throughout her 27 months of service, Nancy had not allowed herself to think beyond tomorrow's flight. She wrote no letters home. She lived only in the present and gratefully flew everything she was assigned to fly. Now her passion—her need to fly those hot airplanes—would have to be channeled elsewhere. She knew she needed to readjust her life's goals; not start over, but start fresh, and she dreaded it.

"Let it burn!" Nancy hollered. Then the Alabama-born Miss Batson let out a rebel yell: "Let it burn!"

The morning of December 20, Betty wrote: "*No water, no heat this a.m. because of the fire. BOQ 14 was like a barn!*"

By evening only six remained on base. "*Richey and I had a steak dinner in the grille then spent the evening packing. All I have to do tomorrow is close up the files and deliver them to Central Files. We wired President Roosevelt and the Army's top commander General Marshall today offering to ferry ships for $1.00 a year!*"

The following afternoon, Betty left for home, Bud, and the children. It was December 21, the longest night of the year. Betty wrote in her diary:

"*McGilvery and her husband were driving up to his parents' home in Smithtown and offered to take my baggage. I came up on the train. The McGilverys got here with my bags about 10:30 and we conflabbed 'til after 1 a.m.*

"Home for good."

December 22, Betty wrote: "*Back to the domestic life again, after over two years! Sort of hard to revive the old interest in marketing, etc., after delivering P-38s and P-47s all over the USA. Nonetheless, I went to market this a.m. and into town with Bud.*

"Home all evening."

✛ ✛ ✛

Epilogue

FLYING REMAINED AT THE CORE OF BETTY GILLIES'S LIFE.

Bud had left Grumman and accepted a position with Ryan Aeronautical, so the family moved to San Diego in early 1945. That spring Ryan hired Betty as a flight instructor. In that position, she flew Ryan's new FR Fireball, a combination piston and jet-powered fighter aircraft. The Fireball was the Navy's first aircraft with a jet engine.

Production of the Fireball ceased when the Japanese surrendered August 14, 1945. World War II was over.

✝ ✝ ✝

Betty Huyler Gillies, a charter member of the Ninety-Nines, the Organization of Women Pilots, was elected president of the organization in 1939 and served a two-year term. During that time, she frequently took to the podium to encourage her fellow members to polish their flying skills and up their ratings to be ready to serve, if needed, in the war nearly everyone was expecting.

During those two years, Betty also oversaw the establishment of the Ninety-Nines' Amelia Earhart Memorial Scholarship Fund. The AE awards are "for members to advance in training and education in aviation and aerospace, including scholarships to complete additional pilot certificates and ratings, jet-type ratings, college degrees and technical training." To this day, AE scholarships are available to Ninety-Nines members.

One of Betty's key efforts as Ninety-Nines president was her pursuit of impartiality in the treatment of pregnant women aviators who needed to keep their ratings current. The CAA classified pregnancy as

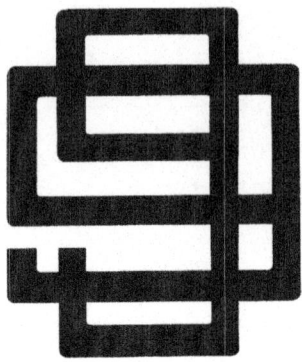

The Ninety-Nines logo *Courtesy: The Ninety-Nines,
the International Organization of Women Pilots*

a "physical deficiency." No distinction was made between pregnancy
and other physical conditions.

The result: The pregnant pilot's medical certificate was ren-
dered invalid and she lost all her ratings because she could not "stay
current," as required by the CAA. For a professional pilot, this
meant loss of the ability to make a living until all her ratings could
be restored—an expensive and time-consuming prospect.

> "Pregnancy is not an abnormal condition," Betty wrote.
> "A pregnant woman is not a sick woman, she is usually in
> excellent health, and she would not fail in a physical exam-
> ination due to eyesight, hearing, lungs, heart or any other
> factor considered in a regular CAA physical examination."
> She suggested a woman's ability to fly be left to the discre-
> tion of her own obstetrician. "A girl should be permitted to fly
> while she is pregnant." By then, Betty had lived this herself.
> She had continued to fly through all three of her pregnancies.

The newspapers picked up the story. One headline characterized
Betty as the "Stork's Copilot." Another said she "Denies Pregnancy
Hinders Piloting."

Betty didn't win a complete victory, but the CAA did revise the offending section using *"temporary"* physical deficiency, which allowed a woman to fly dual with another licensed pilot in order to log the necessary hours to maintain her certification.*

Keeping her Ninety-Nines membership active after WWII, Betty became one of the 10 founding members of the Ninety-Nines' San Diego Chapter in 1946. Then in 1952 she helped her fellow WASP friends BJ Erickson London and Iris Cummings Critchell charter the Long Beach Chapter.

From 1952 to 1961, Betty chaired the All-Woman's Transcontinental Air Race (AWTAR), begun in 1947 by a group of Los Angeles–area Ninety-Nines. Some had served as WASP. The 1929 Powder Puff Derby—the First Women's Cross-Country Air Race— was the inspiration for what became the AWTAR. And the term "Powder Puff Derby" often was used by the press when referring to AWTAR in articles around race time each year.

Betty flew the AWTAR six times. She and BJ Erickson London flew the race together twice, placing second in 1949 and fifth in 1952. Betty retired as race chair following the 1961 race.

Betty's insight into the world of women's aviation made its mark. On May 4, 1964, President Lyndon Johnson announced the formation of the Women's Advisory Committee on Aviation. Betty was one of the 27 nongovernment members appointed. Nearly everyone on the committee was a Ninety-Nines member.

Betty remained an active Ninety-Nine throughout her life. She continued to fly until well into her 80s. In the fall of 1998, Betty took her final flight and "flew west."

---

*Author's note: Thank you to Ninety-Nine member Dr. Jacque Boyd, *Winged Women's Words*, for the use of the material as the source of these paragraphs.

Betty seated in a primary glider (May 2, 1930) *Courtesy: Cradle of Aviation Museum, Garden City, New York*

Air Transport Command Civilian Wings worn by the WAFS (opposite). *Courtesy: Author's Personal Collection. Photo by Joe Weingarten.*

"If You Have Flown"

© *Betty Huyler Gillies*

There are no words that can express
The Magic of that wilderness,
That wilderness away up high
Where banks of clouds float softly by
And hide the problems of earth below
But then you know,—
If you have flown.

If you have flown, then you know
The beauty of the world below,
The meadows green, the waters sapphire blue,
You've felt that it belonged alone to you,
And as your ship obeyed your slightest will
You've felt a thrill,—
If you have flown.

For to those who sail the sky above
Comes peace of mind and understanding love,
There is no bitterness in the sky
As gently earth and clouds drift by,
All is beautiful, serene,—
You know exactly what I mean,—
If you have flown.

Betty in the left seat of the Gillies's twin-engine Beech Baron *Courtesy: The Gillies Family Collection*

Aircraft Betty Flew during World War II

L-2B—Taylorcraft single Continental engine, 65-hp. Maximum speed, 85 mph.

L-4B—Piper "Grasshopper"—single Continental engine, 65-hp. Maximum speed, 90 mph.

PT-19—Fairchild—single Ranger engine, 175 hp. Maximum speed, 124 mph; cruising speed, 106 mph. Open-cockpit, low wing.

PT-26—Fairchild—single Ranger engine, 175 hp. Maximum speed, 128 mph; cruising speed, 106 mph. Closed-cockpit, low wing.

BT-13—Vultee "Valiant" (also known as the Vultee Vibrator): single Pratt & Whitney engine, 450-hp. Maximum speed, 155 mph; cruising speed, 130 mph.

AT-6—North American "Texan" C model—single 600-hp Pratt & Whitney engine; Maximum speed 206 mph; cruising speed 145 mph.

AT-9—Curtiss "Fledgling" (also known as the "Jeep")—twin Lycoming engines, 295 hp each. Maximum speed, 197 mph. cruising speed, 173 mph. Used to bridge the gap between single-engine trainers and twin-engine combat aircraft. The AT-9 was part of Betty's P-47 preparation.

UC-43—Beech, single-engine Pratt-Whitney 450 hp, 195 mph.

UC-78—Cessna, twin Jacobs engines, 225 hp each, top speed 175 mph.

B-17— Boeing "Flying Fortress": four Wright Cyclone engines, 1,200 hp each. Maximum speed, 300 mph; cruising speed, 170 mph; range, 1,850 miles; service ceiling, 35,000 feet..

B-25—North American "Mitchell" twin Wright engines, 1700 hp each. Maximum speed, 275 mph; cruising speed, 230 mph; range, 1,200 miles; service ceiling, 25,000 miles.

A-20 (DB-7)— Douglas "Havoc" twin Wright engines, 1600 hp each. Maximum speed 317 mph; cruising speed 230 mph; range of 1,025 miles; service ceiling, 25,000 feet.

A-30—Martin, twin Wright engines, 1600 hp each. Part of Lend Lease, used by British.

OA-14—Grumman "Widgeon" (Amphibian—lands on water or land), two Ranger engines, 200 hp each. Maximum speed 150 mph. Wingspan 40 feet, length 31 feet.

P-38— Lockheed "Lightning" L model—two Allison engines, 1,475 hp each. Maximum speed 414 mph; cruising speed, 275 mph; range 1,100 miles; service ceiling, 40,000 feet. Tricycle gear as opposed to a taildragger.

P-47—Republic "Thunderbolt" (also called "the Jug"); Betty flew several models. Four versions of the D model were built, counting for most of the total production. Maximum weight, 17,500 pounds. One Pratt Whitney engine, 2,430 hp. Maximum speed 433 mph; cruising speed, 350 mph. Range 1,030 miles. Service ceiling, 42,000 feet. Wingspan, 40 feet 9 inches; Length, 36 feet 2 inches. (Stats from the United States Air Force Museum Aircraft Brochure, Page 21, 2003 edition.) Taildragger.

P-51—North American "Mustang" C model—single Packard-built Rolls-Royce "Merlin" engine, 1,695 hp. Maximum speed, 425 mph; cruising speed, 275 mph; range 1,000 miles; service ceiling, 41,900 feet. Taildragger.

P-61—Northrop "Black Widow" C model—twin Pratt-Whitney engines, 2,100 hp each. Maximum speed, 425 mph; Cruising speed, 275 mph; Range, 1200 miles; Service ceiling, 46,200 feet. Wingspan, 66 feet; Length, 49 feet 7 inches; Height, 14 feet 8 inches. Tricycle gear.

✢ ✢ ✢

During WWII Betty flew two single-engine fighter aircraft that were not part of her WASP ferrying. Both flights were the result of her flying as an employee of two different aircraft companies: Grumman Aircraft prior to joining Nancy Love's WAFS and Ryan Aeronautical in 1945 after the WASP were disbanded. The aircraft were:

F6F "Hellcat"—Grumman Aircraft. 2,000 hp Pratt-Whitney engine. Grumman built the aircraft for the United States Navy.

FR "Fireball"—Ryan Aeronautical. The Ryan FR Fireball was a mixed-power (piston and jet-powered) fighter aircraft designed by Ryan Aeronautical for the United States Navy during World War II. It was the Navy's first aircraft with a jet engine.

Glossary and Acronyms of WWII Aviation and Military Terms Used

AAB—Army Air Base

AAF—Army Air Forces

AT—Advanced Training; aircraft flown in the third of three-stage flight instruction

ATA—Air Transport Auxiliary (women pilots attached to the British Royal Air Force)

ATC—Air Transport Command (U.S. Army Air Forces)

BOQ—Bachelor Officers Quarters

BT—Basic Trainer; aircraft flown in the second of three-stage flight instruction

CAVU—Ceiling and Visibility Unlimited; no clouds above or below the aircraft to impair visibility

Ceiling—Vertical distance from ground to cloud cover

Commercial License—A federal certificate that allowed a pilot to carry passengers for hire or to haul freight

Control Tower—Tall structure at an airfield where air traffic controllers work to stay in radio contact with pilots in the area, giving them instructions as their planes arrive or depart

CPT—Civilian Pilot Training

FD—Ferrying Division; and FC—Ferry Command, the nickname for the Ferrying Division/Air Transport Command

Instrument Flight Training—Learning to fly when there is no visible horizon or when the ceiling is lower than allowable for visual flying. This is known as IFR (instrument flying rules). Flying with a visible horizon is known as VFR (visual flight rules).

P—Pursuit; designation for pursuit or fighter aircraft, as in P-47

Private License—A federal license earned by a pilot who has demonstrated sufficient skills to be allowed to carry passengers, but not for hire

PT—Primary Trainer; the first stage of three-stage flight instruction of military flight training in WWII

RAF—Royal Air Force (British)

RON—Remain Over Night

Transition—Instructing a pilot on how to fly an aircraft in which the pilot lacks experience

USAAF—United States Army Air Forces

WAC—Women's Army Corps

WAFS—Women's Auxiliary Ferrying Squadron

WASP—Women Airforce Service Pilots

WFTD—Women's Flying Training Detachment

WTS—War Training Service (followed CPT, 1941–1944)

Aviation Timeline

Betty Huyler Gillies

1928

November 10—Betty's first flight.

December 23—Betty's first solo.

1929

May 6—Betty earns her Private Pilot Certificate #6525. She has 23 flight hours.

November 2—Becomes one of 99 charter members of the Ninety-Nines, the International Organization of Women Pilots.

1930

Earns Limited Commercial and Transport Licenses.

1939

Is elected president of the Ninety-Nines and serves a two-year term.

1941

December 7—Japanese warplanes bomb U.S. military targets at Pearl Harbor, Honolulu, Hawaii. America enters World War II.

1942

September 10—Betty joins the Women's Auxiliary Ferrying Squadron (WAFS).

September 21—Reports for duty with the WAFS, New Castle Army Air Base (NCAAB), Wilmington, Delaware.

October 23-24—Leads five other WAFS on their first ferrying flight. They deliver six L-4B Piper Cubs to Mitchel Field on Long Island.

1943

January 1—Betty appointed commander of the WAFS Squadron, 2nd Ferrying Group, NCAAB.

March 8—Flies her first pursuit aircraft, a Republic Aviation P-47 Thunderbolt.

August 9—By order of General William H. Tunner, Betty and Nancy Love begin check out on the B-17 Flying Fortress, a four-engine bomber.

August 16—Betty and Nancy both qualify as first pilot (pilot-in-command) of the B-17. They will begin ferrying B-17s.

September 1—Betty and Nancy leave Cincinnati for NCAAB, the first leg of their journey to deliver a B-17 to England.

September 6—General "Hap" Arnold cancels their flight to England. He does not want his women pilots flying into the war zone. Nancy and Betty return to their bases in the United States.

October 1— In Long Beach, California, Betty qualifies in the P-51 Mustang, the United States' fastest—to date—single-engine fighter aircraft.

December 15—In Long Beach, Betty checks out in the twin-engine P-38 fighter. She is the second woman to do so (Nancy Love was the first).

1944

February 5—Betty checks out in the twin-engine Attack plane, the A-20.

April 19–May12—Betty attends Officer Training School (The Army Air Forces' School of Applied Tactics) in Orlando, Florida. The WASP are being prepared to become officers in the U.S. Army Air Forces.

June 6—D-Day, the day the Allied Forces land in Normandy, France. It is the beginning of the Allies' march to victory over Germany, which will come 11 months later.

June 8—Betty is placed in command of the only all-woman ferrying squadron in the Ferrying Division/Air Transport Command, at the Republic Aviation factory in Farmingdale, Long Island (New York).

July 1—Betty is the first woman to check out in the P-61 Black Widow, a twin-engine night fighter.

September 6—Betty is given command of the new WASP squadron opening up at the Republic Aviation Modification Center in Evansville, Indiana. Betty now commands the WASP at NCAAB, Farmingdale, and Evansville.

October 3—Word arrives that the WASP are to be disbanded December 20.

December 14 and 15—Betty delivers five of the newest M model P-47s from Farmingdale to Newark. These are her final pursuit deliveries.

December 20—The WASP are sent home. Betty closes up the WASP presence at NCAAB.

1945

May—Betty flies the Ryan Aeronautical FR Fireball as an instructor. The FR Fireball is a mixed-power (piston and jet-powered) fighter aircraft designed by Ryan for the U.S. Navy during World War II. It is the Navy's first aircraft with a jet engine.

1946

September—Betty is one of 10 charter members of the San Diego Ninety-Nines Chapter.

1952

September—Betty is named chairman of the All-Woman's Transcontinental Air Race (AWTAR).

1961

September—Betty steps down as the AWTAR chairman.

1964

May 4—President Lyndon B. Johnson appoints Betty to his Women's Advisory Committee on Aviation.

1976

July 24, Betty Huyler Gillies was one of ten Charter Ninety-Nines honored by having plaques bearing their names embedded in the Memory Lane section of the walkway that winds through the International Forest of Friendship, Atchison, Kansas (Amelia Earhart's birthplace). The Forest was a Bicentennial (200th birthday) gift to the United States of America.

1977

July 1 to 4—Betty and BJ team up again for the final AWTAR to be flown.

Betty receives a Paul Tissandier Diploma from the Fédération Aéronautique Internationale. The diplomas are awarded to those who have served the cause of aviation—private and sporting aviation in particular—by their work, initiative, devotion, or other endeavors.

1982

Betty receives the Elder Statesman of Aviation Award from the National Aeronautic Association of the United States.

Bibliography

Published Sources

Churchill, Jan. *From Delaware to Everywhere: New Castle Army Air Base, New Castle County Airport*. Dover, DE: Dover Litho Printing Co., 2007. (Partial funding was provided by the Delaware Heritage Commission.)

Churchill, Jan. *On Wings to War: Teresa James, Aviator*. Manhattan, KS: Sunflower University Press, 1992.

Fahey, James C. *U.S. Army Aircraft, 1908-1946 (Heavier-Than-Air)*. New York: Ships and Aircraft, 1946.

Gott, Kay. *Women in Pursuit: Flying Fighters for the Air Transport Command Ferrying Division during World War II*. McKinleyville, CA: K. Gott, 1993.

Granger, Byrd Howell. *On Final Approach: The Women Airforce Service Pilots of W.W.II*. Scottsdale, AZ: Falconer Publishing Company, 1991.

Jessen, Gene Nora. *The Powder Puff Derby of 1929*. Naperville, IL: Sourcebooks, Inc., 2002. (I suggest reading the entire book. It's a great story and resource on the early women who flew. Betty Gillies is mentioned on page 261.)

Keil, Sally Van Wagenen. *Those Wonderful Women in Their Flying Machines: The Unknown Heroines of World War II*. New York: Four Directions Press, 1990.

Kerfoot, Glenn. *Propeller Annie: The Story of Helen Richey*. Lexington: Kentucky Aviation History Roundtable, 1988.

La Farge, Oliver. *The Eagle in the Egg*. Boston: Houghton Mifflin, 1949.

Matz, Onas P. *History of the 2nd Ferrying Group, Ferrying Division, Air Transport Command.* Seattle: Modet Enterprises, Inc., 1993. (Sponsored by the Wilmington Warrior Association.)

Rickman, Sarah Byrn. *Finding Dorothy Scott: Letters of a WASP Pilot.* Lubbock: Texas Tech University Press, 2016.

Rickman, Sarah Byrn. *The Originals: The Women's Auxiliary Ferrying Squadron of World War II.* Springboro, OH: Braughler Books, 2017.

Rickman, Sarah Byrn. *WASP of the Ferry Command.* Denton: University of North Texas Press, 2016.

Scharr, Adela Riek. *Sisters in the Sky*, vol. I and II. Gerald, MO: Patrice Press, 1986.

Tunner, William H., and Booton Herndon. *Over the Hump: The Story of General William H. Tunner, the Man Who Moved Anything Anywhere, Anytime.* New York: Duell, Sloan and Pearce, 1964.

United States Air Force Museum. *Aircraft Brochure: Featuring over 175 aircraft of the U.S. Aircraft Museum with Aircraft Photos, Text, and Specifications.* Newly revised edition, 2003.

Verges, Marianne. *On Silver Wings.* New York: Ballantine Books, 1991.

Government Historical Studies, WWII

"History of the Air Transport Command, Women Pilots in the Air Transport Command." Prepared by the Historical Branch, Intelligence and Security Division, Headquarters, Air Transport Command in accordance with ATC Regulation 20-20, AAF Regulation 20-8, and AR 345-105, as amended. Unpublished. **Author, Lt. Col. Oliver La Farge**, official historian for the Air Transport Command. This is the accepted history on the women ferry pilots of the ATC.

"History of the Air Transport Command: Women Pilots in the Air Transport Command." Historical data prepared by the Historical Branch, Intelligence and Security Division, Headquarters, Air Transport Command in accordance with ATC Regulation 20-20, AAF Regulation 20-8, and AR 345-105, as amended. WASP Archival Collection, Texas

Woman's University Library, Denton, Texas. (This is an abstracted version of the volume listed immediately above.)

"Women Pilots in the Ferrying Division, Air Transport Command." A history written in accordance with AAF Regulation No. 20-8 and AAF Letter 40-34; unpublished. **Author, Capt. Walter J. Marx**, official historian for the Ferrying Division. The Nancy Harkness Love private collection. A copy is also in this author's files.

"Women Pilots AAF, 1941-1944." Army Air Forces Historical Studies: No. 55. March 1946. This document is part of the WASP Archival Collection, Texas Woman's University Library, Denton, Texas. It also is part of the Jacqueline Cochran Collection, Dwight D. Eisenhower Presidential Library, Abilene, Kansas.

Oral Histories

Transcript: An Oral History: Betty Huyler Gillies—Women's Auxiliary Ferrying Squadron. Interviewed by Dawn Letson, director, the Woman's Collection, Texas Woman's University (TWU), October 6, 1996. On file in the WASP Archives, TWU.

Transcript: An Oral History: Betty Huyler Gillies—Women's Auxiliary Ferrying Squadron. Interviewed by author Rob Simbeck, September 1996 and used with his permission. On file in the WASP Archives, TWU.

Transcript: Oral History: Barbara Jane (BJ) Erickson London, WAFS, interviewed by the author, Sarah Byrn Rickman, March 2005. On file in the WASP Archives, TWU.

Transcript: Oral History: Gertrude Meserve Tubbs LeValley, WAFS, interviewed by the author, Sarah Byrn Rickman, December 2004. On file in the WASP Archives, TWU.

Author's personal interviews with:

Nancy Batson Crews, WAFS

Iris Cummings Critchell, WASP

Phyllis Burchfield Fulton, WAFS

Teresa James, WAFS

Gertrude Meserve Tubbs LeValley, WAFS

Barbara Jane (BJ) Erickson London, WAFS

Barbara Donahue Ross, WAFS

Barbara Poole Shoemaker, WAFS

Florene Miller Watson, WAFS

In addition, the author has conducted personal interviews with approximately 60 WASP as part of the WASP Archives Oral History project, Texas Woman's University.

Eisenhower Library

Jacqueline Cochran Collection

International Women's Air and Space Museum (IWASM) Collections:

- Betty Huyler Gillies

- Nancy Harkness Love

- Speeches by Betty Gillies

  "The When, Why, Who, Where of the WAFS" presented at the Southern California WASP Meeting, Laguna Hills, CA, June 14, 1987. The Betty Gillies Collection, the International Women's Air and Space Museum, Cleveland, Ohio.

  "The WAFS (Women's Auxiliary Ferrying Squadron)," presented at the Ninety-Nines, Inc., International Convention Banquet, Baltimore, Maryland, July 27, 1985. From Betty Gillies Collection, IWASM.

The Ninety-Nines Museum of Women Pilots

- Photos

- Ninety-Nines Logo

WASP Archives, Texas Woman's University Collections:

- Betty Huyler Gillies

- Nancy Harkness Love

- Dorothy Scott's letters home, the basis for this author's book *Finding Dorothy Scott*, published in 2016.

- Betty's column "Backward Glance," which appeared in the *Ninety Nines News*, July–August 1970. (TWU)

- Letters from Betty Gillies to Delphine Bohn dated October 18, 1983, to February 8, 1984.

- Archambault/Jernigan collection:

    Letter from Jacqueline Cochran to Air Inspector, dated September 29, 1943. Subject: Lack of Flight Qualifications, WASP, BHG F3 #2 (1264-65), Bolling AFB, Washington, DC.

In the Author's Possession:

Esther Manning Rathfelder's diary excerpts from 1944, courtesy of her daughter, Julie Shively.

Republic News, August 1944 issue, "WASP Assigned to Ferry Thunderbolts from Indiana," from the Gillies family WWII archives.

Note:

WAFS Nancy Batson Crews and I met several times in her home between June and December 2000. We were working on my first book, *The Originals: The Women's Auxiliary Ferrying Squadron of World War II*, which I was writing at her request and with her help. Nancy spent her entire WAFS/WASP career under Betty Gillies's command and thought the world of Betty as both a friend and a leader. I have included in this book some of the things Nancy told me about serving under Betty.

Author's Note

THIRTY-EIGHT WASP lost their lives flying during World War II. Of the 38, three were members of Nancy Love's original WAFS squadron. The deaths of all three are noted in this book.

Biographies have been written about all three. They are:

Daughter of the Air: The Brief Soaring Life of Cornelia Fort
BY ROB SIMBECK,
Atlantic Monthly Press, 1999

Finding Dorothy Scott: Letters of a WASP Pilot
BY SARAH BYRN RICKMAN,
Texas Tech University Press, 2016

Sharpie: The Life Story of Evelyn Sharp, Nebraska's Aviatrix
BY DIANE RUTH ARMOUR BARTELS,
Dageford Publishing, 1996

All three began their WAFS flying at NCAAB under Nancy Love and Betty Gillies in the fall of 1942. Cornelia and Evelyn were transferred to the 6th Ferrying Group, Long Beach, California, in February 1943 where they flew under Barbara "BJ" Erickson's command. Both Cornelia and Evelyn died flying cross-country ferrying missions, Cornelia on March 21, 1943, and Evelyn on April 3, 1944.

Dorothy Scott was transferred to Love Field, Dallas, Texas, on January 1, 1943. She flew for the 5th Ferrying Group under Florene Miller's command. Dorothy died at Pursuit School in Palm Springs, California, December 3, 1943.

All three biographies make good reading. You learn a lot about each of these women.

All three of the original WAFS who died while flying for the Army Air Forces in World War II have a hometown airport named for them:

- Sharp Field—Ord Municipal Airport, Ord, Nebraska;

- Dorothy Scott Memorial International Airport, Oroville, Washington—international because the airport is close to the United States/Canadian border (British Columbia);

- Cornelia Fort Airpark, a small private airport located on the banks of the Cumberland River in Nashville, Tennessee. Unfortunately, the airpark was badly flooded in 2010 and is now part of Nashville's Shelby Bottoms Greenway and Nature Park.

✝ ✝ ✝

Acknowledgments

My heartfelt thanks:

To Doris and Tom Baker at *Filter Press* who believed in me and published *BJ Erickson: WASP Pilot* and *Nancy Love: WASP Pilot* for the audience of young women to whom I hoped the books would appeal. I wanted to reach today's girls with the incredible stories of the women who flew for America during World War II. Doris and Tom and *Filter Press* made that possible.

To Mary Walewski of *Buy the Book Marketing* who is helping me market my books and connect with the wider audience I need to reach to create interest in these books.

To my copyeditor Susan Hindman who came up with the book's incredible title.

To the National Aviation Hall of Fame, Dayton, Ohio, and its director, Amy Spowart. The NAHF awarded me the 2019 Combs Gates Award for my *BJ Erickson* and *Nancy Love: WASP Pilot* books for young readers. The Combs Gates award is for projects that bring to light the accomplishments of the men and women of aviation and space—the human rather than the technical side of aviation. The Combs Gates Award has given me the springboard from which to launch what I hope will be more stories of our outstanding women aviators.

To Vann Nored, a fellow pilot and believer in passing the love of aviation on to the younger generations. Vann enlisted the help of Colorado Springs EAA (Experimental Aircraft Association)

Chapter 72 to support donating my two WASP Pilot books to Colorado Springs area middle and high schools. He works with schools offering STEM classes (science, technology, engineering and math). *Betty Gillies WAFS Pilot* will join the first two books in future distributions.

To the Ninety-Nines, the International Organization of Women Pilots, of which I am a proud member. Several chapters—Fort Worth, Texas, Rio Grande Norte, New Mexico, and my own Pikes Peak Chapter here in Colorado—have contributed funding for my books to be given to young women involved in STEM classes and to Girl Scouts working on their Aviation Badge. And to Terry London Rinehart, BJ Erickson's daughter, who helped us fund this project as well.

And to We Band of Writers, my writing group here in Colorado Springs for helping fund further distribution of all three books in the future.

Betty's story now joins Nancy's and BJ's stories in an outreach to America's young women to bring the world of aviation, science, technology, engineering and math to an ever-widening audience. Nancy Love, Betty Gillies and BJ Erickson were—are—the three women who led the WAFS/WASP of the Ferrying Division, Air Transport Command, World War II.

About the Author

Betty Gillies, WAFS Pilot: The Days and Flights of a World War II Squadron Leader is Sarah Byrn Rickman's tenth book about the women who flew for America in World War II.

Three years ago Sarah switched from writing adult-focused books to writing biographies of these wartime women pilots for the Young Adult market. Why?

"Today's young women need to hear the incredible stories of these gutsy women who broke the gender barrier in aviation. The WAFS, later known as the WASP, paved the way for today's women pilots of the Air Force, Navy, Army, Marines, and Coast Guard."

BJ Erickson: WASP Pilot and *Nancy Love: WASP Pilot*, aimed at this audience, were published by *Filter Press* in 2018 and 2019. For this third book, Sarah is going it on her own. She has established *Flight to Destiny Press* and this biography of Betty Gillies follows the other two.

Age 13 to adult is her new focus. The books are aimed at today's young women as well as their sisters, moms, aunts and grandmothers, who, like the WASP, "look to the stars." Young women—and men—who are seeking future careers in aviation and STEM (science, technology, engineering, math) hopefully will find in these books the inspiration to forge ahead.

A journalist first, Sarah began her career as a reporter/columnist at *The Detroit News* and concluded it as editor of the *Centerville-*

Bellbrook Times, suburban Dayton, Ohio. In addition to writing books, she serves as editor of the *WASP News*, the official newsletter for the WASP Archives, located at the Texas Woman's University Library, Denton, Texas.

Sarah holds a Sport Pilot certificate and flies 1940s-vintage tail-wheel aircraft—like the WAFS and WASP flew back in the day. Her favorite is the Aeronca Champ 7-AC.

Also by Sarah Byrn Rickman

- *NANCY LOVE: WASP PILOT*
  Filter Press, Palmer Lake, Colorado, May 2019 (Y/A biography)

- *BJ ERICKSON: WASP PILOT*
  Filter Press, Palmer Lake, Colorado, March 2018 (Y/A biography)

- *FINDING DOROTHY SCOTT: Letters of a WASP Pilot*
  Texas Tech University Press, Lubbock, September 2016 (biography/nonfiction)

- *WASP OF THE FERRY COMMAND: Women Pilots, Uncommon Deeds* University of North Texas Press, Denton, March 2016 (nonfiction)

- *FLIGHT TO DESTINY, A WASP Novel*
  Greyden Press, Dayton, Ohio, 2014, (fiction)
  Second Edition released March 2017, Braughler Books, Springboro, Ohio.

- *NANCY BATSON CREWS: Alabama's First Lady of Flight*
  University of Alabama Press, Tuscaloosa, 2009 (biography/nonfiction)

- *NANCY LOVE and the WASP FERRY PILOTS OF WORLD WAR II*
  University of North Texas Press, Denton, March 2008 (biography/nonfiction)

- *FLIGHT FROM FEAR*
  Disc-Us Books, Inc., Santa Fe, NM, 2002 (fiction)

- *THE ORIGINALS: The Women's Auxiliary Ferrying Squadron of World War II*
  Disc-Us Books, Inc., Sarasota, FL, 2001 (nonfiction)
  Second Edition released September 2017, Braughler Books, Springboro Ohio

A Note From Sarah

Please visit me on my website: *www.sarahbyrnrickman.com*

While you're there, please click on my Blog link, found to the right of my Flight to Destiny logo at the top. I write a weekly blog dedicated to WASP stories as well as stories of many women flyers of yesterday and today. When I travel somewhere to present my books and my film—*Six WAFS Up Close and Personal*—I write a blog about the adventure.

Click on the **Subscribe** link to receive my biweekly newsletter sent to all my Blog subscribers. Or click on the **Contact** link to send me a message directly. Let me know if you like my books.

What interests you most about the WAFS/WASP?

And thank you for reading my books!

Sarah's Book Awards

2020

- *Nancy Love: WASP Pilot*—**Finalist**, Colorado Authors League, Children's/Young Adult

2019

- *BJ Erickson: WASP Pilot* and *Nancy Love: WASP Pilot*—**Winner, Combs Gates Award**, given annually by the National Aviation Hall of Fame for creative projects that reflect an emphasis on the individual pioneers–the people–who defined America's aerospace horizons. Sarah's two-part series is about women pilots in World War II and is aimed at today's young women readers.

2018

- *BJ Erickson: WASP Pilot*—**Winner**, Sarton Award, Story Circle Network, Young Adult nonfiction:
- *BJ Erickson: WASP Pilot*—**Finalist**, Colorado Authors League, Children's/Young Adult
- *WASP of the Ferry Command: Women Pilots, Uncommon Deeds*—**Winner**: The Marjorie Davis Roller Nonfiction Award, National League of American Pen Women, Inc.

2017

- *Finding Dorothy Scott: Letters of a WASP Pilot*: **Winner**: The Sarton Women's Literary Award in Biography from Story

Circle Network; and also **Winner**, The Colorado Independent Publishers Association (CIPA) Evvy Award in Biography. **Finalist**: The Colorado Book Award in Biography from the Colorado Humanities; the Indie FOREWORD Book of the Year Awards in adult nonfiction/history; and The WILLA Award in scholarly nonfiction given by Women Writing the West. Named for Pulitzer Prize winning novelist Willa Cather.

2016

- *Flight to Destiny*, a WASP novel, **Winner** of the 2016 Eudora Welty Memorial Award in Fiction from the National League of American Pen Women, Inc.

2013

- *Flight to Destiny*, a WASP novel, **Grand Prize, Fiction**, Greyden Press Book Competition.

2009

- *WASP of the Ferry Command: Women Pilots, Uncommon Deeds*, **Winner, Combs Gates Award**, given annually by the National Aviation Hall of Fame for creative projects that reflect an emphasis on the individual pioneers–the people–who defined America's aerospace horizons.

2003

- *Flight from Fear:* a WASP novel, **Finalist**, WILLA Literary Awards, Original Softcover category, presented annually by Women Writing the West.

Printed in Great Britain
by Amazon

62695745R00119